UNDERSTANDING AND TEACHING READING COMPREHENSION

The ultimate aim of reading is not the process of reading the words, but understanding what we read. There has been an increasing emphasis on the importance of reading comprehension in recent years but, despite this, there is very little written on this vital topic accessible to trainee and practising teachers and teacher educators.

Understanding and Teaching Reading Comprehension presents an overview of recent findings on reading comprehension development and comprehension problems in children. It provides a detailed examination of the development of key skills that contribute to comprehension and the characteristics of children who have reading comprehension difficulties, and examines ways in which comprehension can be supported and improved. It is accessibly written for students and professionals with no previous background in the psychology of reading or reading problems.

This indispensable handbook asks the question "what is comprehension?" The authors consider comprehension of different units of language: understanding single words, sentences and connected prose, and outline what readers (and listeners) have to successfully understand an extended text. This book also considers comprehension for different purposes, in particular reading for pleasure and reading to learn, and explores how reader characteristics such as interest and motivation can influence the comprehension process.

To comprehend well, readers need to coordinate a range of skills. These include word reading ability, vocabulary knowledge, syntactic skills, memory and discourse level skills such as the ability to make inferences, knowledge about text structure and many cognitive skills. The authors discuss how each one contributes to the development of reading comprehension, how the development of these skills (or their precursors) in preschoolers provides the foundation for reading comprehension development, and how failure to develop these skills can lead to poor reading comprehension.

Areas covered include:

- word reading and comprehension
- development of comprehension skills
- comprehension difficulties
- assessment
- teaching for improvement

Throughout the text successful experimental and classroom-based interventions are high-lighted. Practical ideas for use in the classroom and summary boxes detailing key points and explaining technical terms are included in each chapter.

Jane Oakhill is Professor of Experimental Psychology at the University of Sussex.

Kate Cain is Professor in Language and Literacy in the Department of Psychology at Lancaster University.

Carsten Elbro is Professor of Reading and Director of the Centre for Reading Research at the University of Copenhagen.

UNDERSTANDING AND TEACHING READING COMPREHENSION

A handbook

Jane Oakhill, Kate Cain and Carsten Elbro

Routledge
Taylor & Francis Group

LONDON AND NEW YORK

First published 2015
by Routledge
2 Park Square, Milton Park, Abingdon, Oxon OX14 4RN

and by Routledge
711 Third Avenue, New York, NY 10017

Routledge is an imprint of the Taylor & Francis Group, an informa business

British Library Cataloguing in Publication Data
A catalogue record for this book is available from the British Library

Library of Congress Cataloging in Publication Data
Oakhill, Jane.
Understanding and teaching reading comprehension : a handbook / Jane Oakhill, Kate Cain, Carsten Elbro.
   pages cm
   1. Reading–Handbooks, manuals, etc. 2. Reading comprehension–Handbooks, manuals, etc. I. Cain, Kate. II. Elbro, Carsten. III. Title.
   LB1050.O215 2014
   428.4'3–dc23   2014009245

ISBN: 978-0-415-69830-6 (hbk)
ISBN: 978-0-415-69831-3 (pbk)
ISBN: 978-1-315-75604-2 (ebk)

Typeset in Bembo
by Wearset Ltd, Boldon, Tyne and Wear

CONTENTS

ILLUSTRATIONS

Figures

Tables

1

WHAT IT'S ALL ABOUT

"Reading without reflecting is like eating without digesting."

Attributed to Edmund Burke, 1729–1797

The purposes of this chapter are:

- to introduce the concept of Mental Models as representations of text,
- to introduce the Simple View of Reading and the distinction between word reading and language comprehension,
- to explain the relation between word reading and reading comprehension,
- to distinguish between poor word readers and poor comprehenders.

The click of comprehension

Reading comprehension is important, not just for understanding text, but for broader learning, success in education, and employment. It is even important for our social lives, because of email, text, and social networking sites. Reading comprehension is a complex task, which requires the orchestration of many different cognitive skills and abilities.

Of course, reading comprehension is necessarily dependent on at least adequate word reading: readers cannot understand a whole text if they cannot identify (decode) the words in that text. Likewise, good reading comprehension will depend on good language understanding more generally. This requires comprehension of the individual words and the sentences that they form. However, comprehension typically requires the comprehender to integrate the sense of these words and sentences into a meaningful whole. To do so, construction of a suitable mental model is necessary. A mental model is a mental representation that is created from information in the real, or an imagined, world – i.e. a gist representation of what the comprehender has read (or heard, or seen). It might, but does not necessarily, include imagery. Try Activity 1.1 to get an idea of how important it is to be able to construct a coherent mental model to make sense of the words and sentences of the text.

You might have guessed what the text in Activity 1.1 is about, but if you are like most of the participants in Smith and Swinney's study (1992), you found it hard to make sense of. Now read the text again, but with the title "Building a snowman". Now you will find that the obscure references, to e.g. *substance*, and turns of phrase *elaborateness of the final product*, suddenly fall into place, and the whole makes perfect sense when you have the appropriate framework for a mental model. Smith and Swinney (building on much earlier work by Bransford & Johnson, 1972) showed that people who were asked to read the above text without a title took considerably longer to read it, and had worse recall of its content, than those who were given the title and were able to use the framework it provided to create an appropriate mental model.

Activity 1.1 The need for a mental model for understanding a text

Read the following short text and try to make sense of it:

> This process is as easy as it is enjoyable. This process can take anywhere from about one hour to all day. The length of time depends on the elaborateness of the final product. Only one substance is necessary for this process. However, the substance must be quite abundant and of suitable consistency. The substance is best used when it is fresh, as its lifespan can vary. Its lifespan varies depending on where the substance is located. If one waits too long before using it, the substance may disappear. This process is such that almost anyone can do it. The easiest method is to compress the substance into a denser mass than it had in its original state. This process gives a previously amorphous substance some structure. Other substances can be introduced near the end of the process to add to the complexity of the final product. These substances are not necessary. However, many people find that they add to the desired effect. At the end of the process, the substance is usually in a pleasing form.

The example illustrates two important points. First, it is very difficult to understand a text without an appropriate mental model. This model may draw not only on titles but also on pictures or, very often, on general knowledge. When information in the text is successfully integrated into a mental model, comprehension "clicks". Perhaps you experienced this "click of comprehension" when you had the title and re-read the text?

The second point is that reading a title or seeing a picture of the situation *after* you have read the text may help only a little. But if you had seen the title before the text, it would have made the text substantially more comprehensible. The point is that a framework for the construction of an appropriate mental representation makes the text much easier to understand, to reflect about, and to remember.

The Simple View of Reading

It is helpful to distinguish between two main components in reading: word decoding and language comprehension. *Word reading* (or decoding) refers to the ability to read single words out of context. *Language comprehension* refers to our ability to understand words, sentences, and text. These are the two key components in The Simple View of Reading (originally proposed by Gough & Tunmer, 1986).

The point of The Simple View of Reading is that variation in reading ability can be captured (simply) in only two components: word reading (decoding) and language comprehension. The name, The Simple View of Reading, is not intended to imply that reading (or learning to read) is a simple process but, rather, that it is a simple way of conceptualising the complexity of reading.

Language
comprehension

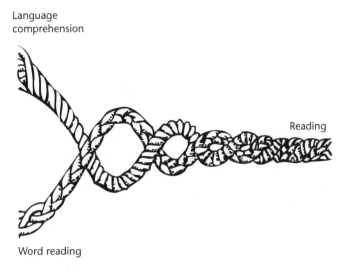

Reading

Word reading

FIGURE 1.1   Skilled reading depends on abilities with both word reading and language comprehension (adapted from Scarborough, 2001).

More precisely, reading ability depends on the product of the two components: Reading = Word Reading × Language Comprehension (R = WR × LC), not just on the sum of the two. This means that if one of the components (either word reading or language comprehension) is zero, overall reading ability will be zero. Thus, if a child cannot read any words or if a child does not have any language comprehension skills, s/he cannot read.

An illustration of the necessity of both components – word reading skills and language comprehension – comes from a story about John Milton's strategy for reading Greek texts after he became blind. Milton got his daughters to learn to decode the ancient Greek alphabet. They were then able to read aloud the texts in ancient Greek to their father, but they could not understand them, because they did not have any knowledge of Greek, whereas Milton could understand, but not decode, the words. Thus, the daughters provided the word reading skills, and Milton provided the language comprehension skills.

The Simple View on development

Although word reading and language comprehension are largely separate skills, it should always be kept in mind that successful reading demands the interplay of both of these skills, and so they both need to be encouraged and supported from the onset of reading instruction. However, the two skills contribute differently to overall reading as the child develops. For the beginning reader, decoding is new, and children differ hugely in decoding ability. Language comprehension, on the other hand, is quite well developed, especially considering the undemanding books that beginning readers are typically presented with. So in beginning readers, the variation in reading ability is almost identical to the variation in word reading.

In the early school years, children need to establish fluent and automatic word reading, which, although not sufficient for good reading overall, is obviously necessary. However, for most children, this is a time-limited task: the child needs to reach the level of competence at which word reading becomes a "self-teaching mechanism" (Share, 1995) (see Box 1.1). The ability to comprehend texts (including the ability to appreciate texts in different content areas and genres), however, is a skill that will continue to develop throughout adult life.

The language comprehension that provides the foundation for reading comprehension develops before children have any formal reading instruction. When they come to school, children are already very competent comprehenders and producers of spoken language without having had formal instruction in these skills (see Box 1.1). Thus, when children become competent at decoding, it is their competence in language comprehension that will determine their overall reading ability. So in more advanced reading, good language comprehension will be more crucial than word recognition.

Box 1.1 The importance of being taught to decode words

Unfortunately, learning to read words does not usually come naturally to children, in contrast to learning to speak. Humans have used speech to communicate for tens of thousands of years, but reading is, in the historical context, a relatively new skill and it is only in the last hundred years or so that the majority of people in Western societies have been able to read and write. Thus there is no reason to expect that the ability to read would have evolved and have innate roots as the ability to speak is generally assumed to (e.g. Pinker, 1994). Indeed, in many cultures still, the ability to read is the exception, rather than the norm. Learning to read is a matter of learning to crack a code.

In English, children need to be taught the relations between letters or letter combinations (graphemes) and the sounds (phonemes) in the language. This is very different from learning a whole new language – it is simply a way of coding the language they already know and speak. This point has an important consequence. There is no logic to the idea that learning to read should come "naturally" to children if they are placed in a literate environment, just like learning to speak. Children learning to read simply have to learn to map the written form of a language they already know well, onto its spoken form. As Gough and Hillinger (1980) put it: Learning to read is an "unnatural act".

Luckily, children do not need to be taught every single written word or all conventions of the orthographic system. The point of the "self-teaching mechanism" (see e.g. Share, 1995) is that children are able to learn to identify new words on their own once they master the basic letter-sounds and how they blend to form spoken words. Of course, in order for the self-teaching mechanism to kick in, children need to be presented with books at an appropriate level for their ability: i.e. books that are sufficiently challenging (with some words that they have not come across before), but not too difficult.

The alphabetic code in English is notoriously difficult, but even the spelling of irregular words, like *island* or *sword*, is far from random. Almost all the letters correspond to sounds in the spoken word, with the exception of one silent letter in each of these words. So these irregularities should not be used as a justification for teaching children by a whole word method. When taught by a whole word method children do not become independent readers unless they extract the letter-sound rules for themselves – which they take an exceedingly long time to do (Brady, 2011; Seymour & Elder, 1986).

Some teachers are concerned that if children are taught by a sounding out/phonics approach, typically using decodable books (which might not have the most exciting storylines), then they might become overly focused on decoding, at the expense of comprehension. However, there is no evidence for this concern. In fact, children who have early, intensive training in phonics tend not only to be better at word reading later, but also to have superior comprehension skills (see e.g. National Reading Panel, 2000).

Even though children typically have a high level of communicative competence when they start school they do not have all the language skills in place that they need for text comprehension. It is a common misconception that, in order to develop competence in reading, beginning readers would need only to be taught to decode the written word, and then their language comprehension skills would kick in and they would be able to understand written texts just as well as they understand oral language. This is a misconception because it ignores the fact that written texts are, in important ways, different from spoken interactions (see "Written vs. spoken language" below), and written texts typically require memory abilities and other cognitive skills that are not so crucial in understanding everyday interactions.

The Simple View on reading difficulties

Recently, the Simple View is often presented schematically, as in Figure 1.2. This representation makes it clear how children with specific comprehension problems can, for example, be differentiated from children who have specific word reading problems (i.e. dyslexics) or generally poor readers (sometimes called "garden variety" poor readers in the literature).

	Language comprehension	
Word reading	Poor	Good
Poor	Generally poor reader	Dyslexic
Good	Poor comprehender	Good reader

FIGURE 1.2 A double dissociation between word decoding and language comprehension. Problems with one component may occur independently of problems with the other.

A consideration of the quadrants in more detail reveals three distinct types of poor reader (though of course in real life, these distinctions might not always be so clear-cut). First, children with dyslexia have severe problems learning to read words. They need much more time and structured instruction than other children to learn the basic orthographic system – how letters typically sound – and how to use the system to blend letter-sounds into recognisable words. Children with dyslexia do not typically have problems with spoken language comprehension. They have difficulties with text comprehension because of their problems with word reading. In many cases of dyslexia, word reading continues to be slow and attention demanding. This puts limitations on the mental resources that could otherwise have been spent on comprehension (Perfetti, 1985) so dyslexics might also have some level of reading comprehension problem.

Poor comprehenders have difficulties with reading comprehension, despite developing good word reading skills and having no other apparent language or cognitive problems. Their problems are not usually apparent or detected before the 3rd or 4th year of schooling, because reading books in the early years are very undemanding in terms of language comprehension plus, as mentioned above, in the early years children's reading competence is typically limited by their ability to read the words. As reading books become increasingly complex, poor comprehenders may experience unexpected reading difficulties (e.g. Catts, Compton, Tomblin, & Bridges, 2012), and their teachers may be surprised and disappointed by the drop in these children's reading abilities. These children with *specific reading comprehension problems*, i.e. the poor comprehenders, will be the focus of much of this book.

Some children have problems with the development of both word reading and language comprehension; they are termed generally poor readers. Children with early language impairments have a higher risk than other children of developing such general reading problems (Bishop, 2001), though the particular combination and extent of the language impairments may also lead to isolated problems with word decoding (Catts et al., 2012).

Activity 1.2 A simple view of your own reading

In your own experience, when have you found yourself in each of the four quadrants of the "Simple View" diagram above? For example, have you experienced being able to decode the words of a text but had real difficulties with comprehension, or not paid attention to the meaning of the text?

*   For each of the three quadrants that represent some aspect of reading difficulty try to list at least one example of your experience as that type of reader.

There are at least four different sets of research findings that support the Simple View:

1   As discussed above, it is possible to have problems with word decoding but not with comprehension, and it is possible to have problems with comprehension but not with word decoding. This pattern is termed a "double dissociation".

2   Research studies have shown that different underlying language skills predict word reading and comprehension in the primary school years, not only within an age group (Oakhill, Cain, & Bryant, 2003), but also across time (Muter, Hulme, Snowling, & Stevenson, 2004; Oakhill & Cain, 2012).

3   As described above, studies have found that decoding and language comprehension are differentially important for reading throughout the school years: decoding is more strongly related to differences between good and poor readers in the early school years, whereas language comprehension is more important in accounting for differences in reading ability later on (Gough, Hoover, & Peterson, 1996, gives an overview).

4   Finally, decoding and language comprehension are selectively associated with other cognitive factors. For example, topic knowledge and depth of vocabulary (how much is known about words) are strongly associated with language comprehension but only marginally relevant for word reading (Gough et al., 1996). On the other hand, size (or breadth) of vocabulary is also important for word decoding because it is easier to decode known than unknown words (Ouellette, 2006).

Activity 1.3 The Simple View can help to gain insight into children's reading

The Simple View of Reading is useful for making well-grounded predictions about children's abilities.

Imagine that one of your pupils has a problem with reading. You give the boy a reading comprehension test (which requires that he answer questions about a text he has just read silently) and find that he is indeed performing a year below age expectancy. You suspect that he might have a problem with word reading, and find that he is even more behind (2 years) on a text of single-word reading.

- Following The Simple View of Reading, what would you predict for the boy's language comprehension? Is it likely to be about a year delayed, like text reading? Would you expect it to be as badly affected as the word decoding of the boy? Would you expect some other level of performance?

Written vs. spoken language

The Simple View raises issues about what is meant by "language comprehension". What is typically meant by "language comprehension" is not the ability to understand everyday spoken language and to participate in conversations about everyday events. Rather, what is intended is the ability to understand texts that were designed to be read – i.e. stories or other texts. This skill is more difficult, and more complex, than understanding everyday spoken interactions or oral narratives, for several reasons:

First, a text cannot be interrogated in the way that a partner in a conversation can be, and it does not adapt in response to a puzzled look or indication of lack of comprehension by the listener.

Second, a written text does not come with all the prosodic information that is so important for the understanding of spoken language, such as intonation patterns. In spoken language, a rising tone can indicate a question. A pause can indicate a change of subject or line of argument. The newcomer to written language has to learn to interpret the meanings of question marks and other punctuation, the significance of paragraphs, headlines, and references.

Third, a written text, even if it is read aloud, is not everyday language – it is a more formal and complex form of language. So, for example, a speaker might say "I've left my handbag in the car, and it's got my reading glasses in it" and not "My handbag, which I left in the car, contains my reading glasses". If the speaker did produce an utterance like the latter, we might say that s/he "talks like a book"! Everyday spoken language does not typically contain embedded relative clauses ("which I left in the car") and has simpler vocabulary ("got ... in it" rather than "contains").

Fourth, written texts are much less anchored in the situation in which they are read than spoken dialogues are. In an oral discussion, words like *here, over there, left, ahead, you, we, now, in a few minutes* (deictic expressions) all make immediate sense because the speaker and the listener share the same situation – the same "context for understanding". Part of the wonder of written texts is that they can convey meaning across time and distance in a way that spoken language often fails to do (see Box 1.2). So, for example, we can read the novels of Jane Austen and can derive a very accurate impression of the lives, concerns, and social milieu of people living in that era. But these wonders come at a price. The price is de-contextualisation: the writer and the reader do not share context. This means that the writer has to carefully define what is here and now, and the reader has to pick up the clues and reconstruct the here and now as part of the mental model of the text.

Box 1.2 Chinese whispers

An example of how spoken text can become distorted is the party game of "Chinese whispers" in which a spoken instruction is passed from one person to another, and becomes distorted as it progresses because of slight mis-hearings and mis-interpretations. A, probably apocryphal, example comes from an era (the 1940s) when military orders had to be sent via a series of radio relays. Each radio operator would listen to a command and then repeat it to the next operator in the series. The story goes that the original order: "Send reinforcements. We're going to advance" had been transformed to: "Send three and fourpence. We're going to a dance", by the time it reached its intended recipient.

Fifth, spoken messages are created on the fly, and so are full of pauses (often filled with "ah", "erm", and "actually"), revisions, repetitions, self-interruptions etc., all signs of the working of the mind of the speaker. By contrast, written language is usually much more dense. For fluent readers, written language carries much more information per word, and per unit of time. The risk is that some points will be lost, even when written language is read aloud slowly.

For these and other reasons, reading a text is more difficult than understanding everyday oral communications. Furthermore, the demands of text increase, and diverge further from the demands of oral communication, as children become older. In particular, there is a shift from "learning to read" in the early years of school (where the emphasis will be on learning to decode and recognise written words, and the texts will be fairly simple linguistically and related to everyday experiences) to "reading to learn" (where the emphasis will be on understanding and learning from increasingly difficult texts). A further issue at this developmental juncture is that background knowledge may be first-hand (i.e. from experience) or second-hand (i.e. from being told, or reading about, situations). Beginning readers probably rely more on their first-hand experience to help them interpret text, and early reading books typically feature characters and storylines that will be close to the reader's own experiences. However, older readers will not only be expected to bring their (first-hand) background knowledge to bear when they are understanding a text, but will also be expected to extract new knowledge from text and then, in turn, use that newly learned information to support further comprehension. As mentioned above, there are some indications that comprehension problems might manifest themselves in some children only once the reading requirements become more demanding, and the emphasis shifts to learning from text, rather than simply understanding texts about familiar situations (Catts et al., 2012; Chall, Jacobs, & Baldwin, 1990; Leach, Scarborough, & Rescorla, 2003).

On the other hand, written texts are open books, not talking heads. Written texts can be browsed, skimmed, skipped, they lend themselves to looking up information, re-reading, and to comparisons across sentences and pages and between texts. Potentially, written texts are much more at the reader's disposal for browsing and selection than is spoken language. However, such non-linear reading requires knowledge of text organisation, of different types of texts (genres), and of strategies to make good use of that knowledge, an issue to which we return in Chapter 5.

Summary

Common sense dictates, and research has found, that the many complex skills in reading can be divided into two categories: those that support word reading (decoding) and those that support language comprehension. The so-called Simple View of Reading maintains that word reading and language comprehension are largely independent sets of skills, but both are absolutely necessary for reading, i.e. text comprehension.

The Simple View of Reading is useful and relevant not only to researchers, but also to practitioners. It makes it clear that the two main components of reading do not necessarily develop in tandem, but that distinctly different approaches may be needed to develop word recognition skills from those that are required to foster the development of text comprehension skills, and that the two components can be assessed separately. One important implication of this perspective is that attention needs to be paid to the teaching of both these aspects of reading. Thus, teachers will need to be aware of not only the cognitive processes that underlie word reading skills, but also those that are important in comprehension.

In recent years, and in particular since the adoption of a "National Curriculum" in the UK (England), a good deal of attention has been given to how to teach children to read words, through the teaching of phonics in particular. Children who fail to learn to read will be identified and given additional teaching. However, although comprehension skills are extensively covered in the curriculum, there is still considerably less attention given to how to teach children to read with understanding, and how to identify children who are having problems with comprehension. As well as being aware of the contributory skills, teachers also need to take account of the specific demands of written language.

Glossary

Reading, **reading comprehension**, and **text reading** all refer to the same thing: prototypical reading for meaning. In the Simple View *reading* means reading with comprehension, that is, the product of *word reading* and *language comprehension*. In daily language, *reading* can refer to many components of prototypical reading, e.g. reading words aloud, interpreting texts or patterns and scales, even clouds and thermometers.

Word reading (word decoding) is the identification of single, written words – either by letter-sound associations or by recognition of the unique letter sequence.

Language comprehension is using identified words to build a mental representation of the contents of a text. In this book, language comprehension is mostly about understanding written language. This ability is closely linked with understanding spoken language.

Suggested answers to activities

Activity 1.1 The need for a mental model for understanding a text
See the main text after the activity.

Activity 1.2 A simple view of your own reading
- Specific problems with comprehension: reading in a second language; reading a text with unknown key words, e.g. about a completely unfamiliar topic; reading a familiar book aloud to a child while thinking of something else.
- Specific problems with decoding: reading degraded, illegible text, e.g. from a screen in sunlight, poor photocopy or very small print, e.g. "the small print" in an insurance document or printouts that have two or four pages of text printed on the same page; reading in a foreign orthography, e.g. Greek or Cyrillic (Russian).
- Combined problems: reading a text (e.g. medical) with long, unfamiliar words about an unfamiliar topic where you have little/no background knowledge.

Activity 1.3 The Simple View can help to gain insight into children's reading
The boy's language comprehension must be much better than his word decoding ability. Otherwise, general reading ability – the product of word decoding and comprehension – could not be *better* than word decoding. In fact, you should expect language comprehension to be at *a higher level than the boy's general reading ability*. There would be no immediate need for intervention against poor comprehension. But you would need to look further into signs of dyslexia.

2
SKILLS AND PROCESSES

"And I've realised something about people who read. People who read: it's not quiet-
ness. It's not passivity. They are having conversations with the writer, with the characters, are part living in that other situation."

From The White Lie, Andrea Gillies (2012, p. 81)

The purposes of this chapter are:

* to explain how mental models are set up though the interaction of input from the
  text and readers' knowledge,
* to introduce the component processes that underpin the representation of text.

The mental model of the text

The importance of language comprehension in reading was outlined in Chapter 1. But
what is meant by language comprehension was not explained nor what processes are
involved in deriving an adequate representation of a text.

It has been known for many years that what readers remember of a text is not the
wording (the "linguistic form") but the meaning. A clear demonstration of this phe-
nomenon comes from the work of Sachs (1967), who was probably the first person to
investigate what people remember from sentences. She asked people to read a series of
sentences, and then tested their memory for them, such as *"He sent a letter about it to
Galileo, the great Italian scientist."* After only a few minutes, people became very unsure
about the exact wording of the sentences they had read, and got completely confused
between the original sentence and others with the same meaning, such as, *"He sent
Galileo, the great Italian scientist, a letter about it."* Or, *"A letter about it was sent to Galileo,
the great Italian scientist."* However, they were still very good at knowing that they had
not read a sentence such as: *"Galileo, the great Italian scientist, sent him a letter about it",*
in which the meaning is changed (so that Galileo sends, rather than receives, the
letter). Thus, Sachs concluded that after only a very short period of time, people forget
the exact way that something was phrased (the "linguistic form") but are still very
good at remembering the meaning. Of course, people are able to remember the exact
wording when it is important (in the case of many jokes, for example) but in general,
they do not.

Thus, a good reader derives an overall representation of the meaning of the text. Some
authors have termed this representation a "mental model" (Johnson-Laird, 1983) or a
"situation model" (Kintsch, 1998) of the text. Though there are some differences between
these two accounts, what they have in common is the view that the representation of the
text goes beyond the literal version. Of course, such representations are derived from
other sorts of input as well – we also have representations of spoken information, of

music and art, and we need visuo–spatial representations of our environment to be able to move around in it effectively. Indeed, the representations might not even be of veridical experiences. For example, when reading we might conjure up images of characters that are not, or not wholly, licensed by the authors (that is why seeing the "film of the book" can sometimes be such a disconcerting experience!). Johnson-Laird talks more broadly of mental models as representations of "the real, or an imaginary, world".

For example, in the text you read in Activity 1.1 in the previous chapter, the text was, at least initially, difficult to understand. However, if you were offered a helpful framework for interpretation before you started reading (e.g. a title or a picture) you would find the text much easier to understand.

In building a mental model of a text, the reader will need to do different things depending on the type of text with which they are confronted. Of course, this model building mostly happens without conscious thought and deliberation in a skilled reader, but to illustrate the sorts of processes that are happening in the reader's mind, we make them more explicit here. In the case of a story, the reader will need to identify the main characters and their motives, since a good deal of the plot of stories revolves around main characters' motives. In the case of informational (expository) text, the reader will need to identify the topic of the text, follow the argument structure, extract the main ideas, and end up with a gist representation of what the text is about. We will discuss in more detail how readers deal with different types of texts (different text genres) later in the chapter. A representation of the language comprehension and word level processes that are important for reading is provided in Figure 2.1.

A reader who is learning from text, in particular, will also need to compare what is in the text with what they already know, and may need to adjust their existing knowledge in the light of the text they have read. This comparison might, in some cases, result in conflicts between prior knowledge and text, which the reader will need to resolve (perhaps by consulting other sources for further information). This skill is termed "comprehension monitoring" and is one of the skills needed for effective comprehension that we discuss below, and in more detail in Chapter 8.

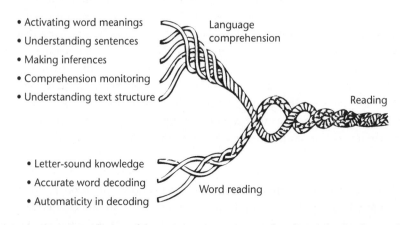

- Activating word meanings
- Understanding sentences
- Making inferences
- Comprehension monitoring
- Understanding text structure

Language comprehension

Reading

- Letter-sound knowledge
- Accurate word decoding
- Automaticity in decoding

Word reading

FIGURE 2.1 An overview of some of the component processes of reading (after Scarborough, 2001). The present chapter introduces the components of language comprehension. Word reading skills are indispensable to reading but they are not the topic of the book.

We now turn to a consideration of the skills and processes that are involved in building a good mental model of a text, that is, in comprehending the text. We will also consider the possible interplay between some of these skills: issues that will be taken up in more detail in later chapters.

Activating word meanings

Obviously, comprehension of a written text will not progress very far if the reader is unable to read the words in it. However, reading words is clearly not enough – the reader also needs to know the *meanings of the words* to make sense of them and, obviously, if a high proportion of the word meanings are unknown (for example, when you are reading a technical text about an unfamiliar topic) then it will be impossible to understand the text as a whole. But, the reader does not necessarily need to know the meaning of every word in the text; some meanings are explained explicitly in the text, and some meanings can be inferred from the context. So, for example, if you read that *"Kevlar is an ideal material for making sails"*, and you have no idea what *Kevlar* is, you can still derive some information about its qualities from the text (it is used to make boat sails) and from your general knowledge. If you consider what sort of material would be good for boat sails, then you might conclude that such material should be both strong and light. Thus, you could infer that Kevlar is likely to have these qualities. Of course, you might be wrong and you almost certainly do not have the full meaning of Kevlar; even as adults, our vocabulary is continuously being improved and refined though reading. As the example shows, it is not a case of "having" vocabulary prior to reading a text; if only a few words are unknown, the text can be used to help the reader to work out or refine the meanings of unfamiliar words.

In addition, it is not just the basic (definitional) meaning of words that is important in comprehension. Vocabulary knowledge is not all or none: there are degrees to which one can know the meaning of a word, a concept that is often referred to as *depth* of word knowledge. The more you know about the meanings of words, the more likely they are to trigger associations that can be important in helping to link up ideas in a text. So, if you read the word *platypus* you might well know that this is an animal, which is native to Australia. What else do you know about the platypus? More in-depth knowledge might include the fact that it is a mammal, has a duck-bill and even more in-depth that, exceptionally, it is one of only two mammals that lays eggs rather than giving birth to live young (the other is the echidna), and one of very few venomous mammals.

Deep vocabulary knowledge is important for building mental models of the contents of texts. This is so because when words are strung together, certain aspects of their meanings are emphasised more than others. For example, the word *blue* usually refers to a certain colour; but it is certainly not the same blue in contexts such as *the blue sky* or *blue jeans*. Indeed, the meaning of *feeling blue* or *blue blood* has little to do with the colour blue. Such contexts highlight select associations to blue, such as "sadness" and "high social status".

Activity 2.1 What is the relevant word meaning?

- What does the word *red* mean in each of these sentences? In which cases are colour irrelevant for good comprehension?
  The British tourists expected all postboxes to be red.
  Their account was deeply in the red.
  The red carpet had been rolled out to receive the successful students.
  Were Lady Macbeth's hands just as red as those of her husband?

These different aspects of vocabulary knowledge, and their relation to comprehension, will be discussed further in Chapter 5. We return to this example, and how such knowledge might support inference making, below.

Understanding and linking sentences

In addition to knowing the relevant meaning of the words of the text, the reader will need to identify sentence structures to interpret how words are related, and to link sentences to each other.

Word order certainly matters. It can make a world of a difference to the mental model whether "the police stopped the young man" or "the young man stopped the police". The two mental models demonstrate that young men are not always the suspects. The difference between the subject and the object of a clause is signalled by word order. Yet, the significance of word order is, in turn, determined by the form of the verb:

> The police stopped the young man.
> The young man was stopped by the police.

The mental models that match these sentences are very similar if not identical even though the surface forms of the sentences differ. Generally, sentences may vary quite a lot at the surface level and still inspire the same mental model: "The police brought the young man to a stop" is a third variant of the same meaning.

As we outlined above, the structure of sentences in written texts is typically more complex than that in spoken utterances. Written texts, for instance, usually have longer sentences and more demanding sentence structures, such as embedded relative clauses ("the dress that the girl sitting on the bench was wearing was red"). Such sentences are often the cause of so-called "garden paths" (initial misinterpretations) especially if the relative pronouns are left out, as in "the horse raced past the barn fell". But even with a relative pronoun, embedded clauses can be difficult. For example, "the man that the woman liked left" is a minor challenge because "left" has to be remembered and combined with "the man" while the embedded information ("that the woman liked") is understood. But while most people (adult skilled readers) can deal with a single embedding ("the cow that the rat frightened jumped"), with the addition of just one more embedded clause sentences become very difficult indeed to understand. Try: "the cow that the rat that the horse chased frightened jumped". Such a sentence has to be consciously unravelled, and understanding it is cognitively demanding. The point is not that we routinely come across such dreadful sentences in written texts, but that understanding the syntactic constructions in written texts can sometimes be quite a challenge, and especially so for children and poorer comprehenders. These issues are discussed further in Chapter 6.

It is clear that a coherent text is more than a list of sentences, the individual sentences need to be connected up into a meaningful whole, and this is where the importance of linking words (text connectives) comes in. Such words can totally change the meaning relation between two sentences or clauses. Compare:

> Dan was very late. He got the bus.
> Dan was very late because he got the bus.
> Dan was very late although he got the bus.
> Dan was very late so he got the bus.

Think for a moment about the meanings of these four sentences and the scenarios they evoke. In the first case, it is not at all clear what the intended link between the sentences is, and you can probably think of various alternatives. In the other three sentences, these alternatives are narrowed down. *Because* suggests that there might have been some other, faster, means of transport (such as a car) or that, perhaps, the bus broke down. *Although* suggests that Dan would not normally have got the bus (but some slower means of transport – walking or going by bike, perhaps) and that he must have been very late to start with since getting the bus did not help much. *So* again suggests that Dan would not usually take the bus, only when he wanted to travel more quickly than usual, but does not carry the same implication as the sentence with *although*, which suggests that his lateness could not be redeemed by catching the bus. Thus, the addition of a connective can imply subtly different variations in meaning that we, as skilled readers, pick up on and appreciate. Of course, these interpretations depend not only on our knowledge of the meaning of the connectives, but also (as is evident from the examples above) on our knowledge of how things work in the world.

Texts are also linked by means of words that refer to the same things across sentences. Such links are inspired both directly and less directly by the text. Here is an example, which will also be relevant in Activity 2.2 below.

> Jane was invited to Jack's birthday party. She wondered if he would like a kite. She went to her room and shook her piggy bank. It made no sound.
> *(Charniak, 1972)*

Jane is the main protagonist here. The reader follows her around and has insight into her thoughts ("she wondered..."). The cohesion of the text and the construction of the mental model of the reader is helped by the consistent use of the personal pronouns *she* and *her* to refer to Jane. For you such anaphoric references between *she* and *Jane* are straightforward, but they may be surprisingly difficult for some children, especially those who have comprehension problems. Such cohesive ties and the use of them in comprehension are further explored in Chapter 6.

Making inferences

Linking personal pronouns to their referents (e.g. *Jane* in the text above) is only one aspect of the reader's processing of the text. There is much more to do to set up a suitable mental model. Far from all the necessary inferences are primed by pronouns or other explicit cues in the text. Readers need to make numerous inferences while reading, to connect up the ideas in the text, and to connect information in the text to what they already know.

Consider the example above. What is Jane thinking of buying Jack as a birthday present? Why does Jane shake her piggy bank? How do you come to those conclusions? What background knowledge are you using?

Before you read on, try Activity 2.2.

Activity 2.2 Your automatic contributions to comprehension

- Without looking back, try to remember which of the sentences below are exactly (*verbatim*) identical to the sentences in the example about Jane at the end of the previous section.

    1   Jane wondered what to give Jack for his birthday.
    2   Jane wondered if Jack would like a kite.
    3   Jane was going to buy Jack a kite for his birthday.
    4   She wondered if she had any money.
    5   She went to her room and shook her piggy bank.
    6   The piggy bank made no sound.
    7   The piggy bank was empty.

- Now go to the end of the chapter and check which ones you got right, before you read on.

To understand the text about Jane and the upcoming birthday party, the reader needs to make inferences based on knowledge of the conventions of birthday parties and money in our culture: the requirement to take a present to a party, the convention of saving money in a piggy bank, and the need for money to buy presents. So, there are certain expectations, and a skilled reader understands that Jane will have the *intention* to buy Jack a present (though there is no mention of a present, or her specific intentions, in the text). Thus, she is not simply *wondering* if Jack would like a kite, she is *planning to buy him one* (as a birthday present). There are other inferences to be made as well: because you know about piggy banks and their characteristics, you know that a piggy bank (typically made of china) will contain (metal) coins and, when shaken, the coins will make a rattling noise, like a castanet. You also know that some rough and ready judgements can be made about the number of coins in the piggy bank, depending on the sound it makes. And if it makes no sound, you might infer that the piggy bank is stuffed with bank notes, but a more likely implication is that it is empty.

We also understand that there are going to be some problems with Jane's plans, and we might also infer how she might feel, and might even begin to predict what might happen next in the story (if it were longer). Thus, in reading this short text, a skilled reader will use background knowledge to support his or her understanding of what is going on in the text and, in particular, the reasons behind characters' actions. Someone (perhaps from a different culture) who did not understand birthday parties, piggy banks, or money would find even this simple story impossible to understand.

Comprehension monitoring

An activity that cannot be entirely independent of inference making is monitoring of comprehension. As skilled readers, we are constantly, even if not deliberately, keeping track of our comprehension and making attempts to remedy it if it goes off track. So, if we misread or miss a word in a text, such that the text does not make sense, we are likely to register this break in the sense and reread a section to see if we made a mistake. Or, if we don't know the meaning of a word in a text, we might try to infer what it means from the context or, if the same word keeps cropping up and we feel that the lack of know-ledge is detrimental to our comprehension (more comprehension monitoring required!) then we might look it up. Furthermore, our monitoring skills might signal that there is a missing link in the text, which requires an inference. Although many inferences will seem automatic and relatively effortless, some will require more deliberation, and the amount of effort required is likely to vary depending on the reader's background know-ledge and experience.

There may also be apparent inconsistencies in a text that need to be resolved. So, for example, if young readers are presented with a short text such as the following, they often do not notice the blatant contradiction, and poor comprehenders have particular diffi-culty (Oakhill, Hartt, & Samols, 2005):

> Moles are small brown animals and they live underground using networks of tunnels.
> Moles cannot see very well, but their hearing and sense of smell are good.
> They mainly eat worms but they also eat insects and snails.
> Moles are easily able to find food for their young because their eyesight is so good.

The children in the study did not know whether or not moles have good eyesight. A reader who had this knowledge would probably find the inconsistency easier to detect because there is not only a contradiction within the text itself, but also a conflict with the reader's prior knowledge. Thus, the detection of inconsistencies in some circumstances will be quite dependent on prior knowledge. In some cases, this may lead the reader to decide to revise their (faulty) prior knowledge – i.e. learn from the text.

Understanding text structure

Comprehension of a text requires more than understanding of the single sentences and how each is related to the next. Comprehension also requires a more general under-standing of how the ideas of the sentences are related. In other words, comprehension requires understanding of the text structure. Structure is important because it can help the reader identify the main idea of a story or other text, and provide a framework for the mental model.

Activity 2.3 Find the structure

The story below has been mixed up.

* Reorder the segments to make the story cohere.
* Which kinds of knowledge did you draw upon to re-order the fragments of the story?

1 The boy asked his mother if she would help fix the TV but she said that he would have to go and buy the newspaper for her first.
2 His mother was pleased with his organisation and stamina, so she made sure that the TV was repaired.
3 Then he went and bought the newspaper.
4 Once upon a time there was a boy who had an old TV in his bedroom.
5 The boy asked for money, and his mother gave him some.
6 The boy was happy to be able to watch TV in his bedroom again.
7 Unfortunately the TV did not work.

The text structure varies according to the type of text. A *narrative* (usually fiction) typically comprises a sequence of causally related events – as in Activity 2.3. It has an introduction with a setting: at the beginning of a story, the reader would expect the characters, or at least the main character, to be introduced. The middle of a story would typically consist of an elaboration of the characters' plans and some attempts to achieve those plans. Stories revolve around characters' goals, which provide reasons for the characters' actions and motivate the temporal and causal structure of events. The end part of a story would typically provide some resolution of the goals and outcomes, perhaps with some evaluation of the characters' attempts to reach his or her goals. Even before they can read, most children have a good understanding of the nature and structure of narrative text (this comes both from being read stories, and from making sense of their everyday experiences), and can narrate simple stories.

A non-fiction (expository) text, however, can have a variety of different structures, such as compare–contrast (Meyer & Freedle, 1984). Typical compare–contrast texts are those that discuss the advantages and drawbacks of things – like taking a loan or solar energy. Or they compare the features of various animals, or household appliances. Such compare–contrast texts often assume that readers will make certain types of inferences, such as evoking the idea of something opposite. If the text, for example, mentions that a particular fridge is relatively silent, by contrast, the reader can be fairly certain that most other fridges are noisier. If women are mentioned as relatively good at multitasking, it is fair to assume that men are not as good at multitasking, since men are the most likely comparison.

Text genres are conventional forms – or text structures – that serve specific communication purposes. For example, email is a genre. At its core it is a personal message, usually about a single topic. It is personal, so you expect it to be from another person and specifically for you. That is partly why spam mail is so annoying, because it is parasitic on your genre-based expectation to receive something personal. Likewise, a book index is a (part of a) genre. It allows you to quickly locate a particular topic. But you do have to know about the conventions of alphabetical ordering and how to use it. News articles are another genre. You expect them to be informative, and to have the gist at the top in the headline, and details later in the text. Again, your expectations are often exploited in advertisements that look like articles, but are in fact written to encourage you buy something.

The role of memory in reading comprehension

Memory is important for the different skills and processes that contribute to reading comprehension, which we have outlined in this chapter. Long-term memory is used to store the meanings of individual words and information about text genre, among other things. As noted above, when this type of information is retrieved quickly and accurately, it can support reading comprehension. For example, someone who can access the meanings of the words in a passage rapidly as they read will find it easier to integrate their meanings into sentences, and someone who can access and use the information about text genre to structure the elements of a passage will find it easier to relate these elements into a coherent whole than someone who lacks such knowledge.

Another type of memory that is important for reading comprehension is called *working memory*. Working memory refers to the systems used to both store and process information while completing a task. The ability to maintain an accurate memory of verbal information, such as the meaning of the sentence that has just been read, and to integrate this with the next sentence that is currently being read, relies on working memory. This type of activity is important for many of the aspects of reading that have been outlined above, such as resolving pronouns and integrating clauses linked by connectives. The ability to hold in memory recently read information to compare its meaning to the next part of the text is clearly also important for identifying when an inference has to be made and to monitor comprehension. Thus, working memory is relevant to many aspects of reading comprehension.

These activities that are key for reading comprehension tap two components of the working memory system proposed by Baddeley and Hitch: the phonological loop and the central executive (Baddeley, 1986, 1996; Baddeley & Hitch, 1974). The phonological loop is dedicated to the temporary storage of verbal information and the central executive coordinates the storage and processing of incoming information. It is this latter aspect of the working memory system that is most strongly implicated in reading comprehension.

Summary

This chapter provides an outline of the different processes that a skilled reader will need to engage in (beyond word recognition) in order to formulate a coherent mental model of the text they are reading as a whole. First, not only must words be recognised, but their meanings and appropriate associations need to be activated in order to help the reader make links between words and concepts in the text. These meaning relations will help to establish links between the sentences and across the text as a whole. Thus, they help in establishing co-reference between sentences (signalled, for example, by the use of anaphoric links such as pronouns, or synonyms, or category–instance relations). They also help to establish coherence across the text as a whole by supporting inferences that relate information in the text to relevant prior knowledge. Making inferences to connect up ideas in a text is crucial to good comprehension. However, although this skill may depend on adequate prior knowledge, there are other factors at work: the relevant knowledge must be activated when needed, and used during the comprehension process. The next skill we considered was comprehension monitoring, and this skill can be used to help the reader identify when an inference is needed. If a comprehender is actively trying to put together information in the text, and finds some inconsistency or gap in their understanding, then that might be a signal that an inference is needed to plug the gap (or, of course, there might be something wrong with the text, or the reader might have misread, or misunderstood, a part of it). In this way, comprehension monitoring can help guide inference making. The last skill we discussed was the ability to use the structure of a text to support comprehension. If the reader has a preconception about how the text will be structured, then that knowledge can provide a framework for their developing mental model, just as appropriate prior knowledge can (as illustrated by the snowman text in Chapter 1).

As we have hinted at in this summary, although we discuss these skills in separate sections of the chapter, and devote a further chapter to each of them, there is substantial interplay between the various comprehension skills. They are mutually supportive in the way that instruments in an orchestra might each have their role to play, but contribute together to an integrated and much richer whole. This is an important point, which we return to in the final chapter of the book.

Glossary

Informational text: This type of text is factual text; sometimes termed *expository* text.

Mental model (of a text): A mental representation of the information in the real, or an imaginary, world. The reader's mental model is developed as the text progresses, and may include information derived from inferences and from background knowledge, as well as what is explicitly stated in the text itself. For instance, if you read the text, *"she opened the drawer and started rummaging through it. Then she tipped out the contents onto the bed"*, you begin to build a mental model of a female person (woman or girl) who is looking for something in a drawer.

Narrative text: A text that is narrated from a particular point of view (the narrator's). Such texts are typically fictional (stories) but sometimes informational texts are written in a narrative form.

Working memory: The sort of memory that is used, for example, when doing mental arithmetic, where certain results have to be remembered while other calculations are made, and then retrieved from memory. For instance, unless you happen to know the answer, you would need to engage working memory to do the calculation 36×17. In particular, working memory is characterised by the need to switch between use of storage and processing capabilities. This sort of memory contrasts with short-term memory, which could be used, for example, to repeat a phone number before dialling it. It also contrasts with long-term memory, which is a more permanent memory store.

Suggested answers to activities

Activity 2.1 What is the relevant word meaning?
- The British tourists expected all postboxes to be red. The word red refers to its core meaning here: the colour red.
- Their account was deeply in the red. The phrase "in the red" means "in debt" here; it can also mean "losing money". Though red numbers are commonly used to denote debt, the colour is not of central importance. It may be replaced by a minus sign.
- The red carpet had been rolled out to receive the successful students. "To roll out the red carpet" means to give someone a very special welcome. Sometimes there may indeed be a red carpet for the special guest to walk on, in which cases the expression does refer to the colour red. More importantly, though, is the reference to a "special welcome".
- Were Lady Macbeth's hands just as red as those of her husband? Again, the word red mainly refers to something else than the colour red. The "red hands" of Macbeth indicate that he "has blood on his hands", which means that he is guilty of the killing of someone (the king). So the question is whether Lady Macbeth is as guilty as her husband.

Activity 2.2 Your automatic contributions to comprehension
- Sentence 5 is the only one that is taken verbatim from the text. All the other sentences *add* something to the original text. If you failed to spot some of the additions, you probably *made them yourself* while you read the text and thought about it. For example, the links between characters and the pronouns that refer to them (*she, he, they*) are made automatically. So after a moment, you have forgotten that you made them, and you may think that the referent, Jane, was mentioned explicitly.

Activity 2.3 Find the structure
- Sentence order 4, 7, 1, 5, 3, 2, 6.
  - Once upon a time there was a boy who had an old TV in his bedroom.
  - Unfortunately the TV did not work.
  - The boy asked his mother if she would help fix the TV but she said that he would have to go and buy the newspaper for her first.
  - The boy asked for money, and his mother gave him some.
  - Then he went and bought the newspaper.
  - His mother was pleased with his organisation and stamina, so she made sure that the TV was repaired.
  - The boy was happy to be able to watch TV in his bedroom again.
- There are signals in the text that it is a classic narrative: *once upon a time*, there is a problem *unfortunately*, and there is a positive outcome *happy … again*. There are also temporal markers, *first, then*, which further support the idea that the text is a narrative.

If the text is a classic narrative, all the conventions of such texts may be relevant, such as an initial problem, attempts to solve it, and a happy ending.

3

ASSESSING COMPREHENSION AND THE CHARACTERISTICS OF POOR COMPREHENDERS

"If you can both listen to children and accept their answers not as things to just be judged right or wrong but as pieces of information which may reveal what the child is thinking, you will have taken a giant step toward becoming a master teacher, rather than merely a disseminator of information."

Easley and Zwoyer (1975)

The purposes of this chapter are:

- to draw attention to the signs of comprehension problems,
- to offer an overview of more or less formal ways to assess reading (or listening) comprehension,
- to increase the awareness of various indicators of test quality.

This chapter is about the signs of comprehension problems – what children with comprehension problems "look like" – and how comprehension problems can be assessed.

Most children's reading comprehension skills develop quite naturally as they are taught to read words, but a substantial minority of children have some level of comprehension problem.

Two readers, two types of problem

Consider the following two transcripts of young children reading a short passage from a reading test (the Neale Analysis of Reading Ability, 1997). A sequence of dots indicates hesitation or failure to read the word following, and words in parentheses show words corrected or provided by the tester.

Box 3.1

George read:

"The lions' final act was in (progress) progress. Jack st- stood … wanting (waiting) waiting to clear the ring. The … thud … thunder outside the circle … no … circus tent had made the lions … rested (restless) restless. Saturday (suddenly) suddenly Tina the lion … tamer (trainer) trainer … st- … (stumbled) stumbled. Her whip fell. The young (youngest) youngest lion sp-… (sprang) sprang to … toward … (towards) her. Jack left … Jack leaped … (swiftly) swiftly inside the cage … cranking (cracking) cracking his whip – that doesn't make sense 'cracking his whip'. Oh yeah ... I get it ... cracking his whip with great ... skill. His ... (prompt) prompt act- ... action ... (enabled) enabled Tina to get (regain) regain control quickly. After that ... brief ... ad- adventure Jack ... decided on (upon) upon his fut- ... future work."

Harry read:

"The lions' final act was in progress. Jack stayed ... stood waiting to clear the ring. The thunder outside the circus tent had made the lions restless. Suddenly Tina the lion trainer stumbled. Her whip fell. The younger (youngest) youngest lion sprang towards her. Jack leaped swiftly inside the cage cracking his whip with great skill. His prompt action ... (enabled) enabled Tina to regain control quickly. After that brief adventure Jack decided upon his further (future) work."

George's reading is painfully slow and full of errors, in comparison with his classmate, Harry, who has few difficulties in reading the words. Clearly, Harry's reading is more fluent: he reads with appropriate intonation, hesitates rarely, and makes few errors. George, on the other hand, reads very slowly and takes more than twice as long to read the story. Decoding is such an effort for George that it seems unlikely that he can also consider the meanings of the words he is struggling to read, or can connect up the sentences to make sense of the passage as a whole. Harry makes only 3 reading errors (*youngest*, *enabled*, and *further*), whereas George makes 15.

After completing the whole test, Harry had a word reading accuracy age 3 months above his chronological age, while George's word reading age was 6 months below his chronological age. After reading the passage, the two children were asked questions about the story they had just read. The questions, together with each child's response, are shown in Table 3.1.

TABLE 3.1 Questions and answers to the lion story

Question	George's answers	Harry's answers
1. Where did this story take place?	Er ... at the circus.	In the circus tent.
2. Were the lions near the beginning, near the middle, or near the end of their act?	Near the end.	Um ... ah (remember?). No.
3. What was Jack waiting for?	To take the lions away.	The lions.
4. Why were the lions restless?	Cos of the storm ... the thunder.	Because ... um ... can't remember.
5. What happened to Tina?	She lost control.	Er ... she stumbled.
6. What did Jack do?	He cracked his whip to get the lions in control.	He whipped the lions (anything else?) He was scared.
7. Who finished the act?	Tina did.	The seals.
8. What did Jack decide after this adventure?	That he would become a lion tamer.	His future work (can you tell me any more?). No, that's all.

The children's responses to the questions give a rather different impression of their reading ability: despite his difficulties with word reading, George gives an acceptable, sometimes quite full and insightful, answer for every question. Harry's fluency is deceptive: although he remembers some superficial information from the story, his other answers are either failures to remember, repetitions of fragments of the wording ("his future work") or confabulations (the seals). Over the test as a whole, Harry's comprehension age is 16 months below his chronological age, whereas George's comprehension is 4 months above average for his age, and well above his word reading age. This further information might lead to a revised impression of which child is the better reader, or at least might lead one to specify more clearly what constitutes "good reading". The above are among the more extreme examples of discrepancies between word reading and comprehension skill, but they are by no means exceptional.

There are several features of the children's answers in Table 3.1 that give insights into differences in their comprehension processes. First, Harry does not *remember* so much about what he has read. For two of the questions, he gives no answer at all, whereas George attempts to answer every question. Second, when Harry does provide information from the text in response, he fails to make appropriate *inferences*. For instance, Harry picks out "his future work" from the text, in response to the final question, but apparently fails to make the inference from the text about what sort of work that might be. George, in contrast, can infer what is intended. Harry's response to question 7 seems to come from his prior knowledge about what might happen at a circus (there might be performing seals) but this response is not licensed by the text (there is no mention of seals). Or perhaps it is simply a linguistic confusion between lions/sea lions/seals. Either way, he does not have a clear representation of what is going on in the story. A further way in which the children's comprehension differs is shown in George's comments to himself as he reads the story. He is obviously *monitoring his comprehension* as he reads because at first he cannot understand the phrase "cracking his whip" as his explicit comment shows (perhaps he initially interprets this as the whip breaking), but then he realises what is meant. This checking procedure is a good indicator of active comprehension, and gives the reader a chance to modify or correct their understanding. Sometimes Harry realises that he has forgotten something, but only when the tester asks him a question.

The transcripts above illustrate the distinction between children who have some difficulties with word reading (George) but good comprehension and those with good word reading but poor comprehension (Harry). It is the latter type of child who is the focus of this book. The examples of Harry's errors illustrate (some of) the typical difficulties exhibited by children with specific reading comprehension difficulties. First, he seems to have a rather literal approach to understanding the text, and when questioned often responds with snippets from the text, rather than an interpretation of what the text means. Second, he shows some indications of vocabulary problems, because he does not seem to know what is meant by "to crack a whip". Third, he does not seem to connect up the text into a coherent whole by making inferences, and fourth, does not obviously use comprehension monitoring strategies to check on and moderate his comprehension. Finally, he is also less good at remembering some of the details from the text, probably because he does not have a representation of the text as a connected whole. These sorts of difficulties are characteristic of poor comprehenders and will be discussed in more detail in the later chapters of this book.

The poor comprehender in the classroom

Intriguingly, children who have comprehension problems are often very competent, even highly fluent, at word reading. But, if questioned about the book they are reading, they might show little interest in talking about it and, if asked specific questions about what has happened in the book or what might happen next, they might be able to provide only a vague answer, or have no response at all. Such children often seem to have rather little interest in reading and books, which makes it all the more surprising that they can often read highly fluently. They do not seem to have particular attention problems – after all, they must have had a reasonable level of attention in order to be able to learn to decode.

The question arises as to whether these children have reading specific problems or perhaps more general language comprehension difficulties. They are not children who have been identified as having a *Specific Language Impairment (SLI)*, though it is certainly true that children with language disorders often have comprehension problems for both oral and written language. Neither do children who have reading comprehension problems have problems communicating orally. However, as we pointed out in Chapter 1, there are many supports available in face-to-face communication, which are not present in text whether it is read or listened to. Yet many studies show that listening comprehension and reading comprehension are highly correlated, particularly once the basics of word decoding have been learned (e.g. Catts, Hogan, & Adlof, 2005). Indeed, the fact that children with poor reading comprehension also show problems with listening comprehension is not surprising, because many of the skills associated with successful reading comprehension are also important for successful comprehension of other media, such as spoken text and even cartoon sequences. The ability to understand stories presented in these media has been shown to correlate in studies of both children and adults (Gernsbacher, Varner, & Faust, 1990; Kendeou, Bohn-Gettler, White, & van den Broek, 2008). This makes sense because processes like understanding and relating events and establishing the relations between events in a text or film to establish local and global coherence are common to all these media. Thus, children with reading comprehension problems might also seem unengaged (or fail to fully understand the plot) when listening to a story being read to the class, or even watching a film or instructional video. The teacher might notice that such children did not voluntarily engage in discussions about a book that is being read to the whole class.

A teacher who suspects that a child has some reading comprehension problems might make an informal diagnosis by trying to engage the child in more taxing discussions about a book they are reading, or asking more generally about whether they like reading and what they like to read. The teacher might also ask the child more diagnostic questions about their current reading book. Typically, children with reading comprehension problems do not have problems answering questions about, or finding the answers to, factual questions about the recent text. Where they do have problems, it is with questions that require them to integrate information from different parts of the text to formulate an answer, or perhaps to integrate information in the text with their knowledge of the world. Such children would also be likely to find it difficult to provide a short summary of the story so far, and might be more likely to just provide a résumé of the last few sentences or page. They would also be likely to find it difficult to predict what might happen next in a story, or how the story might end. Thus, for example, in the case of George and Harry above, we could expect George to predict what the story character, Jack, will go on to do to achieve his goals, whereas Harry, who seems to have little idea about Jack's decision, would probably have great difficulty in coming up with predictions that followed on sensibly from the story.

Sometimes children with good word reading skills, but poor comprehension, are referred to as *hyperlexic* (see Nation, 1999, for a summary of this area). Hyperlexics are defined as having "unusual and premature talent in reading against a background of generalised failure of development, or marked impairment, of other language functions" (Mehegan & Dreifuss, 1972, p. 1106), and their very existence demonstrates that excellent word reading can be accompanied by very poor comprehension. However, unlike poor comprehenders who will be found in mainstream classrooms, such children may also have a range of more general behavioural, intellectual, and/or emotional problems, including ADHD, autism, or general intellectual disability, and so will probably have already been identified as having some special needs.

So, if a teacher wants to confirm his or her informal diagnosis that a child has a specific comprehension problem, how should s/he proceed? Probably by administering a standardised test, to obtain information about how the child's reading skills (both word reading and comprehension) compare with what would be expected of a normally developing child of the same age. That is, the teacher would compare the child's scores to age-related norms from the reading test (but see "How to interpret test scores", later in this chapter). However, standardised reading tests (which we will discuss in more detail below) have limited value beyond an initial diagnosis. That is, they can inform the teacher about the level of a child's reading ability (word reading or comprehension) relative to that of his/her peers, but they do not inform the teacher why a particular child might have comprehension difficulties or how to help him or her.

Of course, one very important process that will contribute to comprehension is the child's word reading ability (see Chapter 1). Many assessments of reading comprehension do not enable a clear distinction to be made between word reading and comprehension problems, because the child needs to be able to read the words in order to have any understanding of the text. In such cases, the teacher could give the child an assessment of listening comprehension – i.e. read test passages to them and ask the child to answer the questions orally (and there is at least one standardised test of listening comprehension available in the UK). Listening comprehension assessments can also be useful for beginning readers, because it is important to know if children have adequate comprehension from the early stages of reading and those who (also) have word reading problems may be overlooked and not receive help with their comprehension difficulties for some years.

There are numerous tests of reading comprehension suitable for a variety of age ranges. However, our intention in this chapter is not to provide a review of such tests but, rather, to outline some key points that should be considered when using a test and interpreting the scores obtained. Not only will such information help with the assessment of children, but it will also help readers of research papers to interpret the assessments used.

Why assess children's reading comprehension?

First, it is important to assess children's progress because the teacher needs to know whether or not a particular child is responding to the teaching, or remediation, provided. It is also important for both the teacher and the student to know whether the aims of the teaching are met. Furthermore, a more specific diagnosis of comprehension difficulties is important so that intervention can be tailored.

Two main categories of assessment are common in schools. These are termed "formative" and "summative" assessments. Formative assessments could be thought of not so much as tests, but more like checks associated with recommendations, where the assessment will inform future teaching and learning. Summative assessments are used to assess achievement, but not in a way that will feed back into teaching: examples would be end-of-year exams or national tests.

These different types of assessment do not necessarily imply different tests, though they might. For instance, formative assessments might be less formal, and perhaps more tailored, assessments of specific skills, but standardised tests could also be used in a formative manner. Thus, a teacher might write comments on a piece of work, including advice about how the work could be improved. An assessment of reading comprehension could be used in an informative (formative) manner if the plan is to use the results to inform a particular plan of action for a child. A combination of these types of assessment might be appropriate in some cases – for instance to assess whether a remediation programme is effective or not (summative), and to make recommendations for further teaching (formative).

Diagnosis of reading difficulties

A fairly obvious reason why a teacher or other educational professional might want to assess reading comprehension would be to determine whether specific children have difficulties and might, therefore, need additional support with their reading. This would typically be a formative assessment: see above. In particular, in the current context, the teacher would be looking for difficulties in text comprehension, but might also want to check that the child does not have word reading difficulties, and that he/she has vocabulary at least within the normal range. In such cases, the expectation would be that the test would provide information about how the child or children differed from children with "average" comprehension. This is usually expressed in terms of a standard score, where 100 is the average, or a "reading age" in years and months, which can be compared with the child's actual age. In this case, there are important considerations about aspects of the test, which will be discussed in the next sections, below. Indeed, given these considerations, teachers might want to administer more than one reading comprehension assessment before being able to confidently make recommendations based on a child's reading ability.

Standardised tests

A first point is that a test must be at the correct level of difficulty, or must be started at an appropriate point if that is an option. If a child performs very well (almost perfectly) on a measure of reading comprehension, then it will not be possible to differentiate that child's performance from that of a number of other children with high scores. Neither is it possible to assess the development of the child with this measure. If the test were more challenging, then it would be possible to see differences in the performance of such children. Thus, we need tests that are sufficiently *sensitive* to differentiate between children. Similar issues will occur if a test is too difficult – there will not be scope in the scores to differentiate between children of different abilities because they all find the assessment very difficult.

A second point is that a test needs to be *valid* – that is, that it measures what it purports to measure. One might think that it is fairly easy to see whether or not a test measures reading comprehension, but the issue of validity is more complex than that. There are two separable aspects of validity: *construct validity* and *content validity*. Construct validity is typically assessed by comparing scores on the test of interest with those from another test, or tests, that purport to measure the same or a similar thing (same construct). So, performance on a new assessment of reading comprehension should be systematically related to performance on established assessments of reading comprehension. This testing of validity is carried out when tests are constructed and is usually reported in the test manual. The issue of content validity concerns the range of abilities that is assessed by the test. For instance, in the previous chapter many of the important components (sub-skills) of reading comprehension were outlined (for instance, vocabulary knowledge, syntactic skills, inference making). Thus, an assessment of reading comprehension could be expected to assess several/all of these different aspects of comprehension in order for it to be considered to have good content validity. A test that assessed only memory for literal information in text would not be considered to have good content validity because it would assess only one specific aspect of reading comprehension. It would probably not have very good construct validity either, because the scores on such a test would probably not relate well to those from other, more subtle, assessments of comprehension. In addition, it would probably be too easy.

A test could also have poor validity because it measures something other than the intended construct (reading comprehension). For instance, if a child could answer even some of the "comprehension" questions without even reading the text, then the test would be, at least to some extent, a measure of prior knowledge rather than comprehension. Try Activity 3.1.

Activity 3.1 Can you guess the answers without reading the text?

Two questions for a text about a pet hamster.

A   Where does Linda's hamster live? In a bed/cage/bag/hat?
B   Why does Linda check the hamster's food tray? To see if it is full/red/empty/cold?

Two questions for a text about smoke alarms in private homes.

C   If you only have one smoke alarm to put up in your home, where should you place it? In the kitchen/in the lounge/near a window/in the bedroom?
D   How often should the battery of the smoke alarm be tested? Once a week/once a month/twice a year/never?

In many reading tests, it is possible to guess the answers to some questions without reading the text first (e.g. questions A and B above). This seriously questions the validity of the tests as a measure of *information gained* from the text.

Questions that are possible to guess may be viewed as measures of the reader's ability to make good use of his or her *background knowledge* and to make inferences. Reading comprehension depends on activation of appropriate prior knowledge, so it may be a good idea to assess whether a reader can do so. For example, when thinking about question C above (where to place a smoke alarm) you may already know that most people die from fires because they suffocate from the smoke while they are asleep. A simple inference from this knowledge would suggest that the correct answer is in the bedroom. However, correct responses to such questions should not be treated as indicators of learning from texts.

Conversely, some questions have surprising answers, such as question D above; the correct answer is once a week. Such questions with counter-intuitive answers may also be useful because correct responses depend on the reader's ability to *overrule* his or her intuition and background knowledge and really *learn something new*. A study of adults in vocational education and training indicated that ability to answer *both* these types of questions was related to educational success (Elbro & Arnbak, 2002).

A third issue is that a test needs to be *reliable*. This is more or less what it sounds like but, as with validity, there are different aspects to reliability. If we are to trust the scores derived from tests, we not only need them to reflect the ability we believe them to be an index of, we also need to know that the test will produce much the same results for the same child if they do it again (so, in other words, that the results are consistent). In the case of standardised reading tests, this is typically assessed by "test–retest reliability" – i.e. giving the same test (or different parallel versions of the same test) to the same individuals at different times. Ideally, the individuals should obtain the same, or a very similar, test score on the two tests (within a short time frame). In the case of assessments that are developed for more exploratory, or experimental, purposes, the inter-item reliability will also be of importance. Measures of inter-item relations are termed the "internal consistency" of the test. This is important in assessing the extent to which all items (or particular groups of items) are measuring the same thing in a test. So, for example, if an assessment contained a group of questions designed to measure vocabulary and a group of questions designed to measure inference skills, we would expect the items within each of those groups to relate well to each other, but not necessarily be related to items from the other group.

To better understand the distinction between reliability and validity, consider palm reading. It is a fairly *reliable* procedure to find the onset of the so-called heart line, for example. People can agree whether it begins below the index finger, below the middle finger, or in the middle – in the case of a particular hand. So, in this sense, palm reading is reliable. However, there is no evidence that it is *valid*, i.e. that the onset of a certain line has anything to do with the degree of happiness or selfishness in a person's love life.

Assessments of reading comprehension: what, how, and how young?

There are various considerations here. First, reading (and listening) comprehension are complex processes, and they involve many different skills and abilities, so which of these should be assessed? Second, different tasks can be used to assess comprehension skills, so which sorts of task should be used? Third, it might be thought that it is not feasible to measure comprehension skills at the very early stages of reading acquisition, because a child's word reading skills will not be sufficiently developed. However, because reading and listening comprehension are closely linked, it is possible to obtain estimates of a child's language and reading comprehension *potential* by other means – the child's ability to answer questions about stories read aloud, short videos, etc.

Which aspects of comprehension should be assessed?

In the previous chapter, we outlined the different skills and abilities that are important to reading comprehension. So, should a comprehension assessment aim to test each of these skills? Ideally, the answer is probably "yes" but, in practice, no assessment is designed to do that. However, there are some major distinctions between types of reading comprehension test that need to be considered in relation to these component skills. There are many tests of vocabulary and, although comprehension and vocabulary are typically quite highly correlated, if vocabulary only were assessed, many important aspects of text comprehension would be missed. Some assessments of comprehension measure comprehension only at the level of sentences. Such components are obviously important to comprehension of texts as wholes because, if a reader cannot understand word meaning and has trouble understanding at the sentence level then, obviously, comprehension of the text as a whole will be compromised.

However, we have evidence that some children can have problems with text comprehension despite age-appropriate vocabulary and sentence understanding (e.g. Cain & Oakhill, 2006). Furthermore, an assessment of vocabulary or a test of sentence level understanding will provide no information about the important underlying skills of comprehension such as the ability to make inferences about events in the text and the integration of information from different parts of a text. At this point, it is appropriate to distinguish between the *processes* and the *product* of reading comprehension. It is the product of reading comprehension that is assessed by a comprehension test: how well the person being tested has understood the text(s) in the test overall. However, the outcome of a comprehension test (typically a single score) tells the tester absolutely nothing about the processes (or deficiencies in particular processes) that resulted in the child arriving at that particular score. Indeed, it is possible for two children to get the same score on a test by very different means (i.e. they might have complementary strengths and weaknesses that will not be apparent from their scores). For instance, one child might have substantial background knowledge that is relevant to the understanding of a particular text, and find that it is easy to integrate the information in the text and answer questions, whereas another child might have little relevant knowledge, but might be very good at making inferences and connecting ideas in the text to learn from it, and might also be good at answering the questions.

The following chapters introduce a number of the processes that are important for adequate comprehension, such as vocabulary, inference making, understanding of text structure, and comprehension monitoring. One or several of these processes might be deficient in children with comprehension difficulties. So, different sets of processes might, in combination, contribute to a particular level of comprehension skill (i.e. the product, or score, on a comprehension assessment). However, in order to help a child with comprehension problems, we need to know not only how they score on a comprehension assessment, but also which particular processes are deficient and in need of support. Thus, if there are concerns about a child's level of reading comprehension skill, it would be good to assess understanding at different levels: word, sentence, and whole text (and perhaps even include some assessments of other skills such as inference or cohesive devices or knowledge about text genre) as the child's pattern of performance on these different assessments may well have implications for the type of help that is offered.

How should reading comprehension be assessed?

The various assessments of reading comprehension have different formats and demands. Some, as indicated above, may require comprehension of only sentences or short passages, whereas others require understanding of longer narratives, factual texts, or even poems. Furthermore, even superficially comparable assessments of comprehension may make different demands on the child. Indeed, recent research (Cutting & Scarborough, 2006; Keenan & Betjemann, 2006; Keenan, Betjemann, & Olson, 2008) has shown that some tests are more dependent on word recognition, whereas others are more dependent on oral language skills.

Whatever the type of test, the child's level of understanding can be assessed in different ways (different response formats), each of which has advantages and disadvantages. These include: open-ended questions, true/false responses, multiple-choice responses, and cloze tasks. Each of these is considered below.

Box 3.2 Four ways to test inference making

The text

Hanna had so many green tomatoes in her garden. They would not be ripe before the frost set in. She wondered whether she could make a kind of jam. She decided to go and buy some nice jars.

Four formats to test inference making
1   *Open-ended question*
    What did Hanna need the nice jars for?
2   *Multiple-choice format*
    What did Hanna need the nice jars for?
    a) To make her kitchen look nicer
    b) To make jam
    c) For her tomato jam
3   *True/false*
    "Hanna decided to buy jars for her tomato jam." True or false?
4   *Cloze task*
    ... She wondered whether she could make a kind of jam. She decided to go and buy some nice _____ (a: jars/b: jam/c: money).
    The words to choose from are a: story appropriate/b: sentence appropriate/c: semantically inappropriate.

True/false judgements. In this format, the child reads or listens to a passage and is then presented with a number of statements, each of which is true or false with respect to the text. The child simply has to make a true/false (or yes/no) judgement about each. This task obviously does not require a complex verbal response from the child and it is also suitable for use in groups or whole classes. But a major disadvantage is that if more subtle aspects of comprehension are being assessed (such as ability to make inferences), then the inferences themselves will be spelled out in the response options. Thus, it will not be clear whether a child gets such a response correct because they are able to make the inference, or because when they see the inference spelled out for them, they realise that is a good option.

Multiple-choice. In multiple-choice tests, the child has to select one response (of a choice of three or four) that they think corresponds to the correct answer. This type of task is somewhat more sensitive than yes/no questions (because there are more response options) but less sensitive than open-ended questions (see below). It is also subject to the same criticism as true/false judgements, in that answers to questions will necessarily be provided as one response option, so that children who do not, for example, naturally make inferences while reading might, nevertheless, *recognise* an inference option as the correct response. Although, as with true/false questions, the child does not need to construct a verbal response, the processing demands of multiple-choice tests can be quite complex since the child has to read and compare the different response options before choosing an answer. One diagnostic advantage of multiple-choice tests is that they can be constructed so that the wrong responses are wrong in consistent and interesting ways. So, for example, in the case of an inference question, the wrong choices could be a different, but inappropriate, inference, and a literal response (as in the jam-making story above, where b) is literal, c) is inferential, and a) is inappropriate). Of course, children might make random choices, leading to errors on such tasks. But, if they consistently choose one type of response (say literal options) over other types of wrong response, this could be taken as an indication that they are too much tied to the literal meaning of the text.

Cloze tasks. In cloze tasks, single words are omitted and have to be filled in by the reader, usually from a choice of 3–5 words. The missing words can be deleted from a passage or from isolated sentences, but for the purposes of testing comprehension of text, a passage should be used. Such tests, like true/false and multiple-choice tests, have the advantage that they can be administered to children in groups.

In the original cloze procedure, every fifth or seventh word is omitted, and readers are requested to guess the missing words. The idea is that the cloze procedure assesses the fit between the text and the reader – and provides results that can be compared across texts and readers. It has been found that readers should be able to correctly provide at least 54% of the omitted words in order for the text to be easily comprehended. The 54% has been shown to correspond to a high (90%) score on comprehension questions. In the range 44 to 54% correct cloze solutions, students will need teacher support to learn from texts. The 44% cloze score corresponds roughly to 75% correct responses to comprehension questions. Below 44% correct, texts are generally frustratingly difficult and not suitable for teaching (Bormuth, 1967). However, these cloze percentages depend to some extent on the age of the readers.

The original cloze procedure relies on the fact that most readability factors correlate. Texts with difficult to guess words are in general more difficult than other texts in many ways at all levels. However, the original cloze procedure was heavily criticised for not being specifically sensitive to aspects of text difficulty above the sentence level. For instance, a study by Shanahan, Kamil, and Tobin (1982) showed that readers (at least, university undergraduates) perform just as well if presented with cloze passages in which the sentences have been scrambled, indicating a sentence-level, rather than a discourse-level, processing strategy.

However, one way to modify the cloze procedure is to delete words that are crucial to the meaning, or to delete particular types of words if the task is devised for a particular purpose (e.g. to assess the child's understanding of connectives specifically) (e.g. Gellert & Elbro, 2013). For example, try the following short cloze task, where a choice of three options is provided in brackets:

> Your skin may become drier during long flights. So you might wish to bring moisturizing cream. Flights may cause other kinds of _____ [dryness/inconveniences/hazards]. For example, many passengers get blocked ears or even a ruptured eardrum.

It is also possible to construct cloze tasks that constitute a coherent passage with options that include sentence-appropriate and story-appropriate words (see Activity 3.2). Snowling and Frith (1986) developed such a task to use with children and found that high-ability readers discriminated between sentence- and passage-level choices, but low-ability readers did not.

Activity 3.2 The cloze format can test very different abilities in reading

- Which abilities in reading are particularly important in each of the examples below?

Consider both word reading and language comprehension abilities. Within language comprehension, some cloze items may be particularly demanding of, for example, vocabulary knowledge, syntactic knowledge, text structure awareness, and the use of background knowledge to support inferences.

A dog named Jazz was swimming in the a) see/cee/cea/sea near b) Oxford/Moscow/ Berlin/Brighton. He was a c) string/strong/struck/strung swimmer. d) And/But/So/ Before the tide was going out, and Jazz was in trouble. He needed to be e) released/ delivered/rescued/liberated. By chance the guard on the pier f) spotted/marked/fed/ patted Jazz.

When words are deleted in such non-mechanical ways, the cloze test can no longer be used as a measure of the readability of texts because each text is treated in a unique way. However, the cloze procedure can still be potentially very useful for testing of components of reading comprehension.

Open-ended questions. Asking open-ended questions is probably the most sensitive way of assessing comprehension, since the child's response is not cued by the various response options. The child simply has to answer a series of questions after reading or listening to a passage of text. Thus, the child can be prompted by the tester to elaborate on a response (by asking, e.g., "can you tell me more?").

Another advantage is that (as with the multiple-choice format discussed above) the child's errors might provide useful insights into his or her problems with comprehension. Like the multiple-choice format discussed above, open-ended questions can be used to reveal systematic processing errors in children's thinking about text, and can be analysed to determine the source of such errors. For instance, Barnes and Dennis (1998) used open-ended questions to explore comprehension in children who had comprehension problems because of neurological disorders. A particularly interesting aspect of Barnes and Dennis's study is that the texts they devised depended on the children having learned a new knowledge base (about an imaginary planet). The children had to learn this knowledge base before reading a set of stories. So, for instance, the children were taught that on this imaginary planet, the covers of books were made of popcorn. They then had to use this information in order to understand the stories and answer questions about them. In one story, this sequence occurs: *"After all this hard work Dack and Tane wanted a snack. They tore the covers off their storybooks and ate them."* The inference question relating to this part of the text was: "What did Dack and Tane snack on?" The answer expected would be "book covers made of popcorn" or just "popcorn". Many of the children with neurological disorders and also a control group of children of normal neurological status, but with comprehension difficulties, had problems answering such inference questions. However, difficulties of the two groups of children seemed to have different sources: the problems of the children with neurological difficulties seemed to stem from their difficulties in retrieving the knowledge-based and text-based information that was fundamental to the inference, whereas the group without neurological disorders was more likely to be able to retrieve the relevant information of both sorts, but to have problems integrating the information to answer the inference question.

An obvious disadvantage of open-ended questions is that at least younger children need to be tested individually, though older children might be able to write their responses. Another disadvantage is that the quality of children's responses is likely to be limited by their general expressive language skills (and their level of explication), so it could be argued that some children might know the correct answers, but might have insufficient ability to formulate their responses fully.

How to interpret test scores

A test score is rarely educationally informative in itself. Test scores need to be interpreted. Above all a test score must be compared to something. If a test is *norm referenced*, the test score can be converted to an age-equivalent score or a grade-equivalent score, that is, the age or grade level at which the particular score is an average score. So, a 9-year-old child may have an age-equivalent reading score of 8 years, which means that the child is 1 year behind in reading.

However, being 1 year behind may not be a problem. It is probably not a problem at the age of, say, 18, because the difference between reading like a 17-year-old and an 18-year-old is marginal. On the other hand, a 1-year lag may be a serious problem for a 6-year-old. This raises the question of what defines a problem when age equivalent scores are used.

The general problem is that it is not at all clear how *a low score* is defined. Compare with the use of a thermometer to judge whether it is too cold in a room or not. The thermometer can measure the temperature but cannot tell when it is too cold. That decision needs human input. Similarly, it is ultimately the teacher or assessor who decides whether a child has a reading problem or not. Reading tests can raise or confirm a suspicion. They do not decide anything on their own.

Some tests are *criterion referenced*. They come with fixed expectations similar to crossbars for high jumps. The outcome is either a pass (get over the bar) or a fail (knock the bar down). The crossbar does not tell how far below the bar or high above the bar the jump was. Many tests in everyday life are criterion referenced: driving tests, tests of alcohol in the blood of drivers, tests to be accepted into the police force etc. However, with respect to reading it is exceedingly difficult to set one criterion that will work for all – or even for children at a certain age. The needs for reading ability are very variable, because texts and reading goals vary according to the particular situation.

Another important source of variation is that school classes differ greatly in reading ability. So if age norms or fixed criteria are used uncritically with no consideration of the child's opportunities to develop, a child may be falsely classified as having a comprehension problem. For example, a typical student in a low-performing class may be classified as comprehension disabled, even though the student has never been exposed to comprehension demanding texts and never had a good opportunity to develop better comprehension.

As pointed out in this chapter, reading tests are important tools for diagnosis of problems. The purpose is not to *classify* children into categories of poor readers, but to help the teacher to make an *informed choice* of texts and activities that are suitable for the child. For example, a child may need some very basic questions and support when inferences are required, but at the same time be very good at locating specific information that is explicitly stated in the text. Matching texts and questions to the child's reading "profile" is a skill, but reading tests and informal observations may help.

Above all, it is important that a child profits from the teaching. Reading tests are a very useful lens, through which one can keep a neutral eye on progress.

Summary

At the end of this chapter, the reader may be feeling somewhat overwhelmed by the numerous test options and formats that might need to be considered. First, it is essential to distinguish between problems with word reading and problems with reading comprehension (though, of course, some readers may have both sorts of problem). But, when it comes to assessing comprehension, there are a number of alternative possibilities, as outlined above. So, how should the teacher or educational professional choose? First, the test needs to be valid (i.e. a test that tests what it claims to test). Second, it should be sufficiently sensitive to differentiate between readers of different ability levels in the age group to be

tested. In general, individually administered tests with open-ended questions will be helpful as diagnostic assessments, and will provide a good deal of information about a child's capabilities and limitations, but of course such tests are time consuming. For a broad-based screening, whole-class assessment, a multiple-choice or cloze test would suffice. It may be that such an assessment could be followed up with more detailed analyses of particular children's problems, if time and resources permit.

Glossary

Test formats:
- *Open-ended questions:* The child should provide answers that are more than just a yes or a no.
- *Multiple-choice:* The child is offered a number of responses and asked to select the best one.
- *True/false:* The child is asked whether given sentences about the contents of a text are true or false.
- *Cloze task:* Every fifth or seventh (or strategically selected) word is replaced by a blank and the child is asked to guess the missing words. Cloze tasks are often of a multiple-choice format.

Test quality:
- *Sensitivity:* The test can reliably differentiate between children of different abilities.
- *Construct validity* means that the test is measuring what it claims or is purported to do. For example, if the test is a test of reading comprehension, it should measure ability to comprehend texts, and not primarily decoding or vocabulary, and thus should correlate well with other well-established measures of reading comprehension.
- *Content validity* means that the test covers the important aspects of reading. If the test purports to test reading comprehension, it should be sensitive to differences in a range of the components that are important for general comprehension ability.

Score evaluation:
- *Norm referenced* means that the test score can be converted to an age-equivalent score or a grade-equivalent score.
- *Criterion referenced* means that a test score can be converted to a pass or a fail.

Semantics: The study of the meanings of words, phrases, signs, and symbols.

Syntax: The principles and processes by which words are put together to form phrases, clauses, or sentences, in particular languages. Note that sentences can be syntactically well formed, such as "colourless green ideas sleep furiously" (Chomsky, 1957) even though they might be nonsense semantically.

Suggested answers to activities

Activity 3.1 Can you guess the answers without reading the text?

A   It is likely that a pet hamster lives in a cage.

B   Linda probably checks the hamster's food tray to see if there is anything in it at all, i.e. if it is empty.

C and D   See the main text.

Activity 3.2 The cloze format can test very different abilities in reading

a) see/cee/cea/<u>sea</u> – is mainly an orthographic choice task, that is, a test of word reading and knowledge of word spellings.

b) Oxford/Moscow/Berlin/<u>Brighton</u> – is a test of background knowledge: which city or town is situated by the sea?

c) string/<u>strong</u>/struck/strung – is mainly a test of accuracy of word reading.

d) And/<u>But</u>/So/Before – tests the understanding of the logical relation between sentences, which is a component in language comprehension.

e) released/delivered/<u>rescued</u>/liberated – is demanding in terms of vocabulary knowledge: what will get the dog out of trouble?

f) <u>spotted</u>/marked/fed/patted – this item requires a proper understanding of the situation, a mental model of the whole situation.

4

INFERENCES
GOING BEYOND EXPLICIT DETAILS TO MAKE SENSE OF TEXT

"For Sale: Baby shoes, never worn."
A six-word story, attributed to Ernest Hemingway, who reputedly wrote it for a bet

"We approached the case, you remember, with an absolutely blank mind, which is always an advantage. We had formed no theories. We were simply there to observe and to draw inferences from our observations."
Sherlock Holmes in The Adventure of the Cardboard Box, by Arthur Conan Doyle

The purposes of this chapter are:

- to point out how the reader must make active contributions to the formation of a mental model of the text – by linking explicit information from the text with relevant knowledge,
- to help distinguish between different kinds of inferences,
- to detail how inferences build on vocabulary and prior knowledge and verbal working memory,
- to present an overview of well-documented ways in which inference making can be encouraged through teaching.

The importance of inferences: an overview

The task of the fictional detective Sherlock Holmes is to reconstruct the motives and the events that led to the murder including who committed it. Holmes collects details and makes inferences to form the most likely coherent story. Similarly, a reader is presented with (more accessible) pieces of information in a text but must form a full mental model of the situation and events by means of inferences and background knowledge. Texts do not usually provide the full overview in a few words, and even when a text comprises only a single sentence (see above), there is still a very rich basis for interpretation and inference making.

Inferences are supported by the text, but they go beyond the information that is stated explicitly. To understand better what this means, consider the following sentence pair: *"Yasmine adored her new pet. The little puppy was very cute and loveable."* The text explicitly states that there was a new pet. Readers do not need to engage in any additional (inferential) processing to appreciate that information. However, a very plausible inference, which does go beyond what is stated explicitly, is that the little puppy was Yasmine's new pet. The text does not actually state this. Knowledge of this state of affairs (that the little puppy was Yasmine's new pet) is only possible if an inference is made to link the content of those two statements.

In many instances, such as the one just described, readers would agree about the inferences that are *necessary* to understand the essence of a text. However, not all inferences are considered necessary for adequate comprehension and, indeed, different readers may draw different inferences. For example, the reader could infer that the little puppy in question had large brown eyes, which is what made it so cute, and that Yasmine had other pets, because this was a *new* pet. However, it is also plausible that the puppy was cute because of its long floppy ears and "new" may simply refer to the fact that this was a recent acquisition. None of these inferences is necessary to construct a coherent representation of these two sentences – the mental model, as described in Chapter 1.

Our example illustrates a critical distinction between different types of inference: some inferences, such as the one that the puppy in the second sentence was the new pet mentioned in the first, are *necessary* to integrate the meaning of the second sentence into the reader's mental model; other inferences can be made by the reader or listener to enrich or embellish their developing mental model, but are not strictly necessary to ensure adequate comprehension (although they may be helpful in some circumstances, as we discuss below). These non-necessary inferences are called *elaborative* inferences.

It is worth noting that the number of possible inferences from a given text is large (perhaps infinite). Therefore, one of the things readers have to do is to constrain inference making to ensure adequate and sufficient comprehension. If readers made all of the permitted inferences from a word or sentence, they might not even reach the second sentence and, more critically, they might make inferences that would be in conflict with ideas presented later in the text. Thus inferences that are merely elaborative, and which do not contribute to the overall coherence of a text, should not be encouraged. It is important to note that whether an inference is necessary or not might depend on where the reader is in a text. Thus, if the text states *"the fighter pilot released a number of bombs over the enemy ship"* an elaborative inference might be that the bombs exploded (and did serious damage to the ship; perhaps even sank it). But that might *not* be the case: the bombs might have been defective, or might have missed the ship and fallen into the sea. However, if the text continues: *"The explosions did serious damage to the ship. . . ."* then an inference is required to link *the explosions* to the previous text, via the inference that the bombs *caused* the explosions. So, at that point, the inference that the bombs exploded has become necessary to understand the subsequent text (but the inference is made backwards, not elaboratively or predictively). It is these sorts of connecting inferences, which help to establish local and global coherence in text, that need to be encouraged and facilitated in young readers.

To examine in more depth the distinction between necessary inferences and those that are purely elaborative, take some time to consider the examples in Activity 4.1.

Activity 4.1 Necessary and elaborative inferences

- Which of the following inferences are necessary and which are elaborative?

    1   My brother fell over in the playground. *Inference:* My brother skinned his knee.
    2   He cut the bread. The knife was sharp. *Inference:* The knife was used to cut the bread.

> 3 She adored her new pet. The puppy was lively. *Inference:* The puppy was her pet.
>
> 4 When Linda turned around she stood face to face with the burglar. She dropped the vase of flowers. *Inference:* The vase broke.
>
> 5 She finished the assignment and handed it in just before the deadline. *Inference:* She was hoping for a good grade.
>
> 6 He was ready for the fancy dress party. The pirate suit was rather special. *Inference:* He wore a pirate suit to the party.
>
> 7 Mum read them a ghost story at bedtime. They left the bedroom light on all night. *Inference:* The ghost story scared them.

Necessary inferences

This section makes a distinction between two types of inference that are both of central importance to text comprehension. They differ in the demands on the reader, hence the distinction is relevant to assessment and teaching.

Local cohesion inferences are the sort of linking inference that is illustrated by the tie between *the puppy* and *new pet*. The reader clarifies the meaning of words and phrases by linking them to other words and phrases in the text. To understand what sort of pet is mentioned in one sentence, it is necessary that the reader links it to *the puppy* in another sentence. This type of local cohesion inference is called a lexical inference because it links lexical items. Similarly, pronouns (e.g. *he, it*) need to be linked to content words to have specific meaning, e.g. *"The boy was sending a message to his friend. It was about a cycling event."* Such inferences are called pronominal inferences. Both lexical and pronominal inferences are necessary to make the text cohere. Their necessity is signalled by a word or a phrase in the text such as a pronoun or a definite reference (*the* pet).

Global coherence inferences are inferences that make the text cohere as a whole. They connect different parts of the text by linking them within the mental model of the text. Typical global coherence inferences are ones that derive the setting of a text or a character's emotions or goals from key words in the text. For example, *"The children paddled and built sandcastles. When the wind picked up they quickly gathered their clothes and cycled home."* A full understanding of this text would require an idea about the setting (at the beach?) and the reasons why windy weather made the children cycle home. Thus, global coherence inferences are necessary for a full understanding of a text.

Whereas local cohesion inferences are always necessary – and often automatic – the need for global coherence inferences depends on several factors: the nature of the inference, the nature of the text, the reading purpose, and the reader. First, readers are more likely to draw inferences about causality than about other relations. For example, when one reads a news article about an aircraft that disappeared, it immediately raises questions about why it happened, and what became of the aircraft. Second, narrative texts inspire inferences about the goals and motives of the characters, because motivation and goals are central to understanding emotions and actions and the plot of the text (van den Broek, 1997). Third, reading purpose is important: there is a substantial difference between skimming for a particular piece of information and reading a textbook to learn about a new topic. If you read a textbook about a new topic and you need to apply your knowledge later, the demands for a coherent understanding and relevant inferences are much higher than if you search only for a specific piece of information. Fourth, there are presumed to be differences between readers' "drive for coherence": that is, their individual expectations for how well connected their mental representation of the text is. Independently of reading purpose, some readers will set their expectations for coherence higher than do others.

As we mentioned earlier, the number of inferences that can be drawn from any given text is numerous. Thus, an important question is how to teach children to draw these necessary inferences. We return to this point in the later section entitled "How can inference making ability be improved?"

How to assess a student's ability to make inferences

There are many different ways to measure children's ability to make inferences, and some ways are certainly more practical in the classroom than others. To find out if, in principle, children can draw a particular inference from a text, you can ask them questions that require an inference to be made after they have read (or listened to) a story. An example of a short story and the types of inference questions that could be asked is provided in Table 4.1.

Another method is to ask the child to retell the story, either orally or in writing. As mentioned in Chapter 2, readers do not remember texts verbatim: they construct a mental model of the text that will include useful inferences that help them to make sense of that text. For that reason, the summary will reflect what information – including inferences – was brought to mind during reading. Such activities are possible even with pre-readers on viewing a picture book (Tompkins, Guo, & Justice, 2013).

As a teacher of reading comprehension, you will have to be able to ask inference-demanding questions both to assess comprehension and to encourage children to go beyond the literal meaning of the text. The next activity provides examples of how to do this.

TABLE 4.1 Types of inference questions

"In the morning, Pauline immediately spotted her friend Susie's new school bag. It was a rucksack type but not a silly pink and childish thing like her own. When her father was back from work, she asked him if she could join him on his shopping trip into town. She knew that there were lots of shops just next to the supermarket (Waitrose) where he always shopped."
    Some inference demanding questions:

- What colour is Pauline's school bag? (a lexical inference)
- What sort of bag is Susie's new school bag (a local cohesion inference)
- What colour bag does Pauline want to get? (an elaborative inference)
- Why does Pauline wish to accompany her father into town? (a global coherence inference about her motivation)
- What sort of shop does Pauline really wish to go to? (global coherence inference)

Activity 4.2 Ask inference-demanding questions

- Read the story below and generate some inference-demanding questions to tap the inference types that were outlined in Table 4.1: lexical inference, local cohesion, and global coherence.

> Most of the inhabitants of Oatby were born there. The place had almost everything: a grocery shop, a pub, a village green for football and little children's feet, a school, a health centre, even a TV and phone shop. But there were no cafes, and few educational opportunities. The number of people was dwindling. House prices were dropping. In an attempt to counteract this development, the town council decided to get in touch with Center Parcs and other holiday centres. The spelling ability of future generations might be endangered, but that would have to be dealt with in due course.

If you ask children questions to tap inference making, you will be able to assess their *potential* to generate an inference, whether they can in principle make an inference. However, you cannot establish if they typically make inferences *as they read* the text. The distinction between the potential to make inferences and spontaneous inference making is important. As explained in Chapter 1, a reader constructs a representation of a text's meaning as they read or listen to a text. Comprehension is a dynamic process: as the reader reads or hears each new piece of information, its content is integrated with the mental model (the meaning-based representation) constructed thus far. Frequently, an inference has to be made to enable this integration to take place, as illustrated in Activity 4.1, and this typically has a small processing cost: it takes time to generate inferences. Therefore, to ascertain whether inferences are made during reading, researchers may record how long it takes to read a critical sentence when an inference is required and compare this to the reading time when an inference is not required, such as this sentence pair where the link is stated explicitly: *"Yasmine adored her new puppy. The puppy was very cute and loveable."*

Timing how long a child takes to read a variety of carefully controlled sentences in passages is not practical in the everyday classroom. A different indicator of whether or not children are generating inferences when reading or listening to text, and also a good way to encourage deeper constructive processing, is the Questioning the Author technique. This may be something that you have tried during whole-class or small-group story reading: stopping and asking children questions such as "why do you think he said that?" and "what do you think will happen next?" With this technique, you focus the child's attention on a specific aspect of the story, such as a character's response or the next stage in the plot. To use this technique to encourage inference making, in addition to assessing whether or not an inference has been made, it is important not to ask simple closed questions (i.e. those that have a simple literal answer, or which can elicit a yes/no response), but instead those that lead to discussion (Beck & McKeown, 2001).

Thus, it is possible for teachers to use a range of techniques in the classroom – summarisation, focused questioning, and the more general questions just discussed – to assess children's inference making ability.

The development of inference making

Inferences are necessary to make sense of the world around us and they are not restricted to understanding text. For example, if we consider autobiographical experiences, we sometimes need to infer why someone reacted in a particular way: the recipient of a gift not being pleased on unwrapping the gift (perhaps a dress that was a size too big!). Because inference making is important for understanding our world, it is not surprising that children make the types of inferences necessary to understand text from an early age, before formal reading instruction begins. However, studies disagree about the level of competence young children appear to have.

As noted above, inference making (and other aspects of text comprehension) can be assessed in pre-readers by reading texts aloud to children. One study used this technique to assess 4- to 6-year-olds' potential to generate inferences. The children were read sentences that described the setting of a story, such as: *"Peter played all day with a bucket and spade."* Children were able to answer questions that tapped their ability to infer the likely location of the story, e.g. "Where did Peter spend the day?", with about 60% accuracy. They were also able to integrate the meanings of sentence pairs such as: *"Peter picked up the bucket and spade. He put the toys in his bag"*, assessed with the question: "Where are the toys now?" (Florit, Roch, & Levorato, 2011). This study demonstrates that young children have the potential to make a range of inferences, but they do not always do so, even when prompted by explicit questions.

One factor that may limit the extent to which children generate inferences is memory, because inferences often require us to remember critical details from different parts of a text (as we described in Chapter 2) and memory improves during childhood. In the study described above, the information was presented in short one- or two-sentence segments before each question, so the memory demands were slight. Even then, children did not make all of the necessary inferences to understand settings and link sentence pairs. However, a typical story contains more than two sentences. When children hear longer, more naturalistic texts, their inference making ability is much lower. A study that demonstrated this included children aged from 6 to 15 years. When children were asked questions after each paragraph in the story, the 6-year-olds answered only one-third of the questions tapping necessary inferences correctly and even the oldest children did not achieve 100% accuracy on the inference-tapping questions (Barnes, Dennis, & Haefele-Kalvaitis, 1996). One factor that explained children's inference making ability was their ability to remember other details in the text: children who were better at recalling explicitly stated facts in the text made a greater number of necessary inferences.

To date, it is not well understood whether there are qualitative changes in the knowledge and skills that help children to improve their inference making with age. However, these studies tell us three important things about the factors that influence children's inference making ability. First, individuals are more likely to make an inference from a shorter than from a longer, more naturalistic text. Therefore, a child's ability to answer inferential questions might be overestimated if they are asked inference-tapping questions after only very short texts. Second, when young children do not make an inference, it may be because they have forgotten critical explicit information in the text. Therefore, if a child fails to make an inference, it is a good idea to check that they remember the relevant facts in the text that support the generation of that inference. Third, inference and memory for explicit details are related: children who are good at making inferences are also good at remembering other facts from the text. This is probably because those children construct more accurate and coherent mental models of texts. For that reason, it is a good idea to assess memory for the important details in a text, as well as child's inference making skills.

Another factor that might influence inference making is knowledge, both vocabulary knowledge and background knowledge related to the topic of the text, because many inferences rely on vocabulary or background knowledge. For example, to make the inferences described above, the reader has to know that a child typically plays with a bucket and spade at the seaside and that a bucket and spade are toys. Therefore, perhaps younger children make fewer inferences than older children because they have poorer vocabulary and background knowledge. The way in which vocabulary knowledge can support inferences can be illustrated by returning to the example of depth of knowledge about the platypus, which was used as an example in Chapter 2. If the reader encounters the following text: *"The platypus was reluctant to move. She was curled round the eggs protectively"*, various processes might be set in motion depending on the reader's knowledge. If the reader does not know that platypuses are mammals, then they will probably assume that the platypus is curled round her own eggs, and will link the sentences without problem. If they know that the platypus is an egg-laying mammal, they won't have a problem either. However, if the reader has *some* knowledge about the platypus (that it is a mammal) but does not know that it is an egg-laying mammal then, if they are monitoring their comprehension and actively trying to link up the sentences, they will encounter a problem – "eggs" does not fit with their (limited) knowledge of "platypus" and they have a comprehension problem to resolve. In this case, the reader might do one of two things to resolve the apparent inconsistency – they might infer that, contrary to what they thought, the platypus lays eggs (and is either not a mammal, or an odd one) or they might reason that the eggs the platypus is curled round are not, in fact, her own eggs, but perhaps some taken from a bird's nest, which she intends to eat. Thus, not only the detection, but also the resolution, of inconsistencies will, at least in some cases, be quite dependent on prior knowledge. Finally, the reader might be led to make an inference, which later turns out to have been incorrect, so that their mental model has to be revised later.

The role of background knowledge in inference making has been examined by Barnes and colleagues, in the study with the 6- to 15-year-olds we mentioned above (Barnes et al., 1996). In this study, children learned a novel knowledge base about an imaginary planet, Gan. They were then presented with a story in which necessary and elaborative inferences could be made by integrating information in the text with that new knowledge. Inference making was probed by asking children questions. For example, one new piece of knowledge that was taught was that *"The flowers on Gan are hot like fire."* At one point in the story, the characters are walking across a flower meadow when they cry "ouch". To understand the reason for this reaction, the reader needs to link the information in the text (stepping on flowers) with the item in the knowledge base and infer that the flowers could likely burn one's feet.

There were two predictable findings in this study on the role of knowledge in inference making. First, as noted above, inference making improved with age. Second, all age groups made more necessary inferences than elaborative inferences. Thus, it is not the case that younger children are less likely to constrain their inferences to those that are necessary for comprehension. The authors then looked to see if background knowledge could explain why inference making improved with chronological age. They checked whether or not children had learned the essential knowledge needed to answer each inference-tapping question and then controlled for this knowledge when calculating success at inference making for each child (basically they disregarded answers to questions when the child could not recall the relevant knowledge base information). As might be expected, the younger children were more likely to forget some of the newly taught knowledge than the older children. However, the older children still made more inferences than the younger children even when these differences in retention of the knowledge base had been taken into account.

Thus, it seems that knowledge per se may not explain age-related improvements in inference making. One factor that did make a difference was speed of access to the newly taught knowledge base: how quickly children could recall these facts when prompted. Speed of access predicted the ability to make a necessary inference up to the age of nine. Thus, younger children in particular may fail to make necessary inferences when they are slow to activate the relevant background knowledge.

These studies of early inference making demonstrate the importance of both memory and ease of access to relevant background (or vocabulary) knowledge. One thing to note is that, for different age groups, different types of information may support inference making (and text comprehension, in general). For example, in young children's books there are often illustrations. When an illustration supports an inference required to make sense of story events, it facilitates inference making in children up to 9 years of age; from 9 years onwards, children's performance is not facilitated by helpful illustrations – they can draw these inferences just as readily from the text alone (Pike, Barnes, & Barron, 2010). In addition, children are able to make inferences to understand narratives that are not presented in words (e.g. cartoon sequences or videos). Work looking at the foundations of reading comprehension has assessed children's understanding of multi-episodic picture books and shown that, if they were asked questions about the "text", children as young as four could make inferences about a character's feelings, the causal relations between events, the theme of a story, and also generate predictions, and that this predicts their later reading and listening comprehension skill (Lepola, Lynch, Laakkonen, Silvén, & Niemi, 2012; Paris & Paris, 2003). Thus, inference-making skills can be fostered and assessed through shared storybook reading from an early age. We will return to this point in the later section on how to support and develop inference making.

Difficulties with inference making: who has difficulties with inference making and why?

There is a large body of evidence that children with reading comprehension problems do not generate as many necessary inferences as their peers. Here we consider the three most prominent reasons for poor comprehenders' problems with inferences: poor memory, access to knowledge, as well as how able a reader is to set appropriate standards of coherence for reading. But first, we need to review why inferences are so critical to the construction of a mental model.

In Chapter 2, we described the product of successful comprehension: a mental model which is a representation of a text's meaning, in which information from different parts of the text is combined and also related to relevant background knowledge. Children with poor reading comprehension do not engage in the same level of integrative and inferential processing as good comprehenders to combine the meanings of successive sentences that is needed to ensure coherent and full understanding of a text's meaning.

To examine these issues in more detail, first we will consider a study of 7- to 8-year-old children with either good or poor reading comprehension (Oakhill, 1982). These children were presented with short three-sentence texts such as the following: *"The mouse ate the food. The food was bread. The mouse looked for some cheese."* If you integrate (or combine) the meanings of these sentences, the statement *"The mouse ate the bread"* is an accurate inference from this text and, critically, it maps onto the mental model that you have constructed for this short text.

One way to test if such inferences are made is to see whether children (or adults) later mistakenly "recognise" statements that are components of this mental model, but which were not presented earlier. For example, the statement *"The mouse ate the bread"* is congruent with the mental model, whereas the statement *"The mouse ate some cheese"* is not. Although the latter may be a possibility, it is not constrained by the information provided in the text: the text does not state that the mouse found any cheese, which is why this statement is not congruent with the mental model. Children with poor reading comprehension are less likely to differentiate between these two types of statement: those that are congruent with the mental model and those that are not (Oakhill, 1982). Studies such as this suggest that poor comprehenders are less likely to engage in the processing needed to construct a coherent and accurate representation of a text than good comprehenders.

Poor comprehenders are also less likely to engage in another type of inference that is necessary to build a coherent mental model. As we stated earlier, an inference involves going beyond the information provided explicitly in a text. Sometimes, quite important details such as a character's age or the specific setting of a story are not stated explicitly, but there are strong indications provided in the text. Take the example provided above: *"Peter played all day with a bucket and spade."* Because of the likely setting for playing with this equipment, a plausible inference is that Peter spent the day at the beach, but the text does not state this. Poor comprehenders are less likely to make this type of inference than good comprehenders (Cain & Oakhill, 1999).

So, why do children with poor reading comprehension make too few inferences? Here we consider three potential sources of difficulty with inference making: memory, knowledge, and the reader's standard for coherence.

Memory. When we discussed the development of inference making we noted the importance of memory skills. As shown in Chapter 2, children with poor comprehension skills have weaker memory capacity than children with good comprehension. In particular, they do poorly on memory tasks that go beyond simply remembering lists of words or numbers; their ability to process information while storing previously read or heard information is weak. It is easy to see how this type of memory supports inference making when the reader (or listener) is trying to link information between different sentences in a text and/or additionally recruit background knowledge to make sense of implicit details. Take a look at Activity 4.3 and think about the different types of memory that support the reader's ability to answer the questions.

Activity 4.3 Memory demands

Some inferences are difficult because they span a large part of a text. The reader will have to keep something in mind that was read much earlier in order to make an inference. The risk is that the earlier information is forgotten. Hence, memory demands are an important factor for the difficulty of inferences and questions that require inferences.

- Take a look at the following questions and try to rank order them in terms of how memory demanding they are. How much text has to be kept in mind before each of the inferences can be made and the questions answered?

> Linnea got up early, eager to greet the new day. She enjoyed everything. She enjoyed her busy schedule – Monday scouts' club, her Wednesday badminton, and Friday chess evenings. Even her after-school paper rounds on the other days were fun now that it was spring and the weather was warm. She already knew some of the people on her paper round. Today, she hoped to see the "cat lady" who had vaguely promised her one of the new kittens. Linnea got out into the kitchen and found a notice on the work surface next to her bowl. She read "Please, could you buy some milk for tea on your way back from badminton. Love, mum".

- Which days of the week does Linnea do paper rounds?
- What day is it (if her mother is right)?
- How did she first meet the "cat lady"?
- Will Linnea see the "cat lady" today?

Once you have analysed a text and considered how memory is so vital to inference making, it comes as no surprise that independent measures of memory (such as those described in Chapter 2) predict inference making ability in typically developing readers (Cain, Oakhill, & Bryant, 2004). For children with poor comprehension skills, memory is particularly predictive of their performance when the inference involves integrating information in sentences separated by several additional sentences, as shown in Activity 4.3. The pattern of performance on inference questions that tap information that is close together and information separated in the text is shown in Figure 4.1.

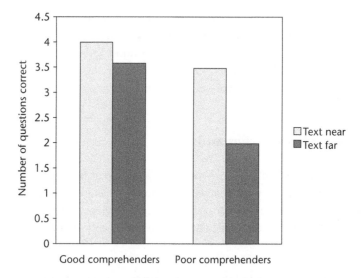

FIGURE 4.1 Less-skilled comprehenders have particular difficulties making inferences that require the combination of information across several sentences in a text.

Since it is difficult to train memory capacity as such, it is important to find other ways to support poor comprehenders. One such way is to help poor comprehenders to engage in activities as they are reading that support the construction of mental models of the text contents to help to minimise the effects of poor memory. It is much easier to understand and to remember text that fits well into a developing mental model. Another way is to use graphic models and other memory aides. We discuss both of these in the later section on "How can inference making ability be improved?"

Vocabulary and background knowledge. Vocabulary and background knowledge are important for inference making. In the initial example, the inference that the new pet was a puppy is only signalled if the reader knows that a puppy is a small dog and therefore an example of a likely pet. Clearly, even very simple inferences can be made only if the reader has the requisite background knowledge. However, as we discussed earlier, developmental studies have demonstrated that speed of activation of knowledge, rather than knowledge per se, is critical in explaining age-related differences: older readers think of relevant information more quickly than younger readers. How do knowledge and access to that knowledge relate to poor comprehenders' inference making difficulties?

We have examined the role of background knowledge using the technique of teaching children about the imaginary planet Gan, which was described earlier. When knowledge is carefully controlled for in this way, poor comprehenders still make fewer inferences than good comprehenders (Cain, Oakhill, Barnes, & Bryant, 2001). In other work, we have also found that even when poor comprehenders fail to make an inference they often have the relevant background knowledge when questioned directly (Cain & Oakhill, 1999). Thus, it seems that, as with young readers, inferences are not made simply because poor comprehenders lack background knowledge.

Similar to younger readers, poor comprehenders may be too slow at thinking of relevant knowledge to be able to make use of this knowledge when reading: fast and accurate access to the meanings of words and background knowledge is required if it is going to be available to be used during comprehension. When looking at single words, there is evidence that poor comprehenders are less likely to activate related words. For example "bed" and "dream" are both associated with sleep, so you may readily activate these words when you read about someone sleeping. Although such knowledge is well established even in young readers, children with poor reading comprehension are less likely to spontaneously make the connection (Weekes, Hamilton, Oakhill, & Holliday, 2008). Thus, it is likely that poor comprehenders are also less likely to activate related words and knowledge when reading a connected text and, for that reason, knowledge relevant to inference making may be less readily available. It may be that when processing text, poor comprehenders typically activate only a narrow meaning of a given word and thus do not have broader attributes of that word and associates of the word readily accessible. This suggests that some factors that influence inference making are not necessarily under our automatic or conscious control. It also suggests that poor comprehenders may need to work more consciously with associations to key vocabulary in the texts before and during reading.

Inference making ability is not only relevant for reading comprehension; it is also a cornerstone in vocabulary acquisition. The study on generating inferences from picture books found that inference making abilities when children were aged 4 years predicted their vocabulary knowledge 1 year later, which predicted their listening comprehension (Lepola et al., 2012). This speaks strongly to the need to foster inference skills, not only because of their importance for understanding extended text, but also for their importance in developing vocabulary knowledge. In Chapter 5 on vocabulary, we discuss the role of inferential skills in vocabulary development in more detail.

Standard for coherence. We have already mentioned that young children do not make as many inferences as do older children and, also, that memory and ease of access to relevant knowledge might play a role in this. Another factor that might influence how readily a reader makes an inference is their *standard for coherence*, which we discuss in more detail in Chapter 8. Certainly, when adults are required to read to study for a test they generate more inferences than when required to read for entertainment (van den Broek, Lorch, Linderholm, & Gustafson, 2001). Thus, it seems that readers (and listeners) set goals, and when it is important to make all of the critical links between information in a text and to derive conclusions from that text, we will do so, as when reading this text. In contrast, when we are reading for pleasure, for example a novel, we may make less deliberate effort because the purpose is to be entertained rather than to learn from the text.

Children who are good comprehenders are sensitive to the stated task goals: when told that they will be tested on their memory for a text's content, they take longer to read it and also remember more of its content compared to a "reading for pleasure" goal; children who are poor comprehenders do not adjust their reading in response to these different goals (Cain, 1999).

In conclusion, it seems that there are, at least, three reasons why inference making might be hard for some children: poor memory, access to knowledge, as well as how able a reader is to set appropriate standards of coherence for reading.

How can inference making ability be improved?

Instruction in how to generate inferences has been included in a range of reading comprehension interventions, some with inference at the core and some in which inference is included as part of a broader package. Because of the variety of different inferences that can be made for any given text, there are a variety of instructional techniques. Here we highlight a few to show the range of support that is possible.

Some interventions have focused on the idea that poor comprehenders lack an *awareness of when inferences are needed* and how to make those inferences. For example, one technique is to show children how to analyse the text for clues. Using sentences such as *"Sleepy Jack was late for school again"*, children can take individual words and explore what information each provides, under teacher guidance. In this example, *sleepy* suggests that the character may have overslept, thus providing a reason for being late for school, *Jack* combined with school suggests that this is a schoolchild and not a teacher who would most probably be introduced as Mr X, and *again* indicates that this has happened before. Such interventions are designed for small-group work. This type of lexical inference activity can then be applied to short stories so that children get practice, in addition to training, in how words provide clues to meaning. This type of training has been administered by researchers to children in small groups and benefited both inference making and broader comprehension skills, assessed by standardised comprehension tests (Yuill & Oakhill, 1988).

The intervention just described also included some instruction in questions to promote inference making, such as *who*, *what*, *where*, and *why*. Other inference interventions have made such questions the focus of the training. In a recent classroom intervention, teachers used one of three questioning techniques: wh-questions, which in this study were: *who*, *what*, *when*, and *where*; causal inference questions, which were specific to each of the texts taught in the intervention; and also a general questioning technique in which every five to six questions, students were asked "How does the sentence you just read connect with something that happened before in the story?" (shortened to "Connect it" once students were familiar with the question and technique). Each method resulted in gains in understanding, suggesting that a range of questioning protocols can be used to get students thinking about text and generating inferences (McMaster et al., 2012).

A third approach uses graphic organisers to make students aware of their own contributions to inferences. Here is an example:

> During the 20th century, fishing boats became hugely more efficient so that it was possible to catch large quantities of fish in a short time. Towards the end of the century it became necessary to regulate fishing, for example by setting limits (quotas) on the catches of each fisherman or boat.
>
> *(from Elbro & Buch-Iversen, 2013)*

An obvious question is *why* it has become necessary to regulate fishing. The answer requires an inference that draws on information *both* from the text *and* the reader's background knowledge, as illustrated in Figure 4.2.

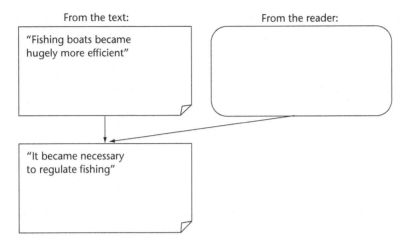

FIGURE 4.2 A graphic organiser can elucidate the contributions from both the text and the reader, e.g. "there is a limited amount of fish to be caught".

In one study, 10–11-year-old students worked primarily with non-fiction texts and causal inferences (why-questions). This work had a strong and significant positive impact on the students' inference making during reading in general – and even a long-term positive effect on their general reading comprehension (Elbro & Buch-Iversen, 2013).

Activity 4.4 Graphic organisers to support inferences

- Draw a graphic model that illustrates the inference needed to answer the following questions. Your model should show which information comes from the text and which the reader has to supply (as in Figure 4.2).

The text: Paula had not seen Margot at school for a whole week. It was so unlike her. But last week Margot had been coughing and sneezing. She wondered whether she should give Margot's parents a call.
Question 1: In Paula's view, why has Margot been absent?
Question 2: What is Paula's role at school?

Summary

We have shown that there are many different types of inference that can be generated from a text. What we think is particularly important to remember, is that this type of deeper constructive processing is not only essential for good text comprehension, but develops from an early age for a variety of media: children strive to make sense of how things connect together. Clearly, good memory and vocabulary and general knowledge are necessary to support inference making, but it may be that we have to ensure that children have rich knowledge bases of information so that critical information is activated and readily available for use in comprehension when reading or listening to text. That may help to minimise the influence of weak memory on reading comprehension. Other methods to encourage and support inference making involve the use of graphic organisers, which can help to make clear the connections between different information in the text. All of these methods encourage children to be more active processors of meaning, so they may prove useful to drive both inference making ability and its automaticity.

Glossary

Inference:

*   *Local cohesion inferences* are a sort of linking inference: they specify the meaning of words by linking them to words in adjacent sentences, e.g. *the girl* < *she*. Local cohesion inferences are *necessary* to make the text cohere. They are signalled by a word or phrase in the text such as a pronoun (e.g. *she*) or a definite reference (*the* house) in the text.
*   *Global coherence inferences* are inferences that make the text as a whole cohere. They are both required to produce a mental model of a text and are also determined by the mental model. Typical global coherence inferences are used to derive the setting of a text or a character's emotions or goals based on indications in the text. Global coherence inferences are *necessary* for a full understanding of a text, but they are influenced by the goal of the reader and other factors.
*   *Elaborative inferences* are further associations and guesses about the contents and development of a text; they are *not necessary* for understanding the text. For example, they may contribute to the feeling of suspense during reading of fiction. In many cases, however, they are detrimental to comprehension because they lead the reader away from the course and gist of the text.

Suggested answers to activities

Activity 4.1 Necessary and elaborative inferences
*   Which of the following inferences are necessary and which are elaborative?

    1   Elaborative.
    2   Necessary, instrument.
    3   Necessary, identity.
    4   Elaborative, but very likely.
    5   Elaborative, possibly a causal inference.
    6   Necessary, the suit was the fancy dress.
    7   Necessary, a causal inference.

Activity 4.2 Ask inference-demanding questions
Some inference-demanding questions are:

*   *Where would you go to buy milk in Oatby?* Answer: to the grocery shop. This is a local cohesion inference from *milk* to *grocery shop* – a lexical link.

- *Where would you go in Oatby to buy milk on a Sunday?* Answer: the grocery shop is likely to be shut, so the best bet might be to find a petrol station somewhere in the vicinity. This answer requires a couple of knowledge-based inferences.
- *What sort of place is Oatby?* Answer: a village. This answer can be made by means of a *global coherence inference* based on the number and sorts of shops and institutions in Oatby.
- *Why is the population of Oatby dwindling?* Answer: because there are not enough jobs. This answer is based on a *local cohesion inference* from "no job opportunities".
- *What age group is leaving Oatby?* Answer: young adults. This is based on a more *global coherence inference* because it has to take into account information from different parts of the text. It is most likely to be the younger generation because there is a lack of cafes and educational opportunities that young people will be looking for.
- *Why is it suggested that the spelling ability of future generations might be endangered?* Answer: because of the spelling of *Center Parcs*. This answer requires a *local cohesion inference* – to make sense of the final line of the text by referring back to the penultimate sentence.

Activity 4.3 Memory demands

- *Which days of the week does Linnea do paper rounds?* Answer: Tuesdays and Thursdays. The answer requires combination of information from two adjacent sentences, but there are five weekdays to keep track of which adds to the memory load.
- *What day is it (if her mother is right)?* Answer: Wednesday. This response almost certainly requires that the reader go back through almost the whole text. This is probably the second most memory demanding of the questions.
- *How did she first meet the "cat lady"?* Answer: probably on her paper round. The answer only requires combination of pieces of information from adjacent sentences. This is the least memory demanding of the questions.
- *Will Linnea see the "cat lady" today?* Answer: not if her mother is right. This answer requires pulling together information from the beginning (Wednesday badminton), the middle (the cat lady is one of the customers on Linnea's paper round), and end of the text (back from badminton). Thus, this question is the most memory demanding.

Activity 4.4 Graphic organisers to support inferences

- *Question 1:* In Paula's view, why has Margot been absent?
  From text: coughing and sneezing. *From reader*: those are symptoms of a cold or the flu.
- *Question 2:* What is Paula's role at school?
  From text: give parents a call. *From reader*: teachers should check with parents when students are absent. Conclusion: So Paula is probably a teacher.

5

KNOWING AND LEARNING THE MEANINGS OF WORDS

Lisa was reading *The Butterfly Lion* by Michael Morpurgo (p. 12). She read slowly: *"She scrutinised me from under the shadow of her dripping straw hat."* She did not get it. What did *scrutinised* mean? Lisa took a chance and read on: *"She had piercing dark eyes that I did not want to look at."* Oh, so this woman stared in a piercing manner! Lisa had learned something about a new word.

The purposes of this chapter are:

- to underline that a good vocabulary is indispensable for good reading comprehension. Yet, good reading comprehension is the most important source of vocabulary knowledge,
- to focus on the importance of vocabulary depth and inference making rather than just the number of words that children know,
- to suggest ways in which teaching may simultaneously further both growth in vocabulary and reading comprehension.

Vocabulary and comprehension: a two-way street

It is clear that effective reading comprehension depends on good knowledge of the meanings of words. Indeed, for a long time it has been known that vocabulary knowledge is strongly related to reading comprehension (Carroll, 1993; Davis, 1944, 1968; Thorndike, 1973). A reader may be able to read all the words out loud but may not understand the text anyway, as in this example: "Spin relaxation proceeds conventionally, independent of the annealing protocol, in the ferromagnet" (example from Scarborough, 2001). To understand the example, the reader needs special word knowledge from physics including *spin*, *relaxation*, *annealing*, and *ferromagnet*. Some estimates are that about 90% of the words need to be known for the reader to have a good chance of understanding a text (Nagy & Scott, 2000).

However, it is not usually necessary to know all the words in a text, or to stop to look up all unknown words because, to some extent, their meanings can be worked out from the context (as in the example at the beginning of this chapter). New vocabulary items are learned, and existing vocabulary is refined, through reading, even in adulthood. Indeed, it is widely thought that, once children become fluent readers, then written text is a major source of new vocabulary (Cunningham, 2005; Nagy & Scott, 2000). In fact, as is pointed out in more detail below, there is evidence for reciprocity between vocabulary development and reading comprehension: each has a beneficial effect on the other.

It is usually possible to work out at least an approximate meaning of a new vocabulary item, as in: *"It [the house] overlooked a* bayou *lined with gum trees, its waters thick with lime green duckweed and ringing with the sound of mallard and wood ducks"* (Connolly, 1999). If you did not already know the meaning of the word *bayou*, a reasonable inference from the context would be something akin to swamp or marshland.

Here is another example. Perhaps you know what a *dugong* is, or perhaps you have a vague idea, but know very few details about dugongs. Here is some information about dugongs:

> The dugong has been hunted for thousands of years for its meat and oil. Traditional hunting has great cultural significance throughout its range. The dugong's current distribution is reduced and disjunct, and many populations are close to extinction.
>
> *(Wikipedia, 28 June 2013)*

So, by now you should have realised (if you didn't know already) that a dugong is an animal, and a rare one at that. If you read on in Activity 5.1, you will get some clues as to what sort of animal and its natural habitat.

Activity 5.1 The two-way street between vocabulary and comprehension

- What can you learn about dugongs from this text?
- Which words are unknown to you? Which of these unknown words are likely to be the most important for understanding the passage?

> Like all modern sirenians, the dugong has a fusiform body with no dorsal fin or hind limbs, instead possessing paddle-like forelimbs used to manoeuvre. It is easily distinguished from the manatees by its fluked, dolphin-like tail, but also possesses a unique skull and teeth. The dugong is heavily dependent on sea grasses for subsistence and is thus restricted to the coastal habitats where they grow, with the largest dugong concentrations typically occurring in wide, shallow, protected areas such as bays, mangrove channels and the lee sides of large inshore islands. Its snout is sharply downturned, an adaptation for grazing and uprooting benthic sea grasses.

Another example of this interaction between word (and world) knowledge and reading comprehension can be seen in ambiguous words. Many words in English are ambiguous in that they have more than one meaning. Thus, a single word might have two or more dictionary definitions such as *spade*, which can mean very different things: a digging implement or a playing card. The intended meaning can be worked out from the text context, and the meanings of other words in that context, when it is available. Thus, the meaning of a sentence such as: *"He picked up the spade"* is ambiguous. But if the next sentence is: *"The digging would be good exercise"*, then the intended meaning becomes clear.

The resolution of ambiguous words provides a good example of the interactive nature of text comprehension: the reader's current mental model can provide the context for the interpretation of such words, and that is what would typically happen in normal skilled reading.

The examples, including Activity 5.1, illustrate two points, one for each of the ways in which vocabulary is related to comprehension:

The first point is that vocabulary knowledge is crucial for comprehension. If you did not know or could not work out what a dugong is, you would have only a very sketchy understanding of the paragraph above. You would also have trouble understanding *further information on the same topic*, such as "one of the main causes of population decline is fishing-related activities" or "They can go six minutes without breathing".

The second point is that it is possible to glean at least some knowledge of words from their context. Even though the meaning of a word may not be explained but taken for granted, the reader can often infer at least something about it.

The mutual relationship between vocabulary and comprehension means that readers can enter either virtuous or vicious circles. With limited vocabulary knowledge, comprehension may suffer, and the new vocabulary knowledge gained may be minimal. Conversely, a skilled reader with relevant prior knowledge and vocabulary may learn a lot from the same text. For example, the further information that dugongs cannot stay underwater indefinitely, but have to surface to breathe, is evidence that they are not fish, even though fishing is a source of population decline. These positive or negative circles – referred to as the "Matthew effect" (Stanovich, 1986) – are discussed in more detail in the section on reading experience below.

Vocabulary: breadth, depth, and access

What does it mean to know a word? To explain this is probably as complicated as explaining what it means to know another person. Most people know both people who live in their street and their own best friend. What they know about these two is vastly different. They may know *of* and a bit *about* their neighbours and may recognise them when they meet them. Knowing their best friend is a completely different and infinitely richer and more profound matter. Similarly, knowing a word spans all the way from the most superficial recognition – "I think I have heard the word *benthic* before, but I am not

---

Activity 5.2 How deep is your knowledge of these words?

- How much do you know about each of these words: *table, maroon, auspices, quator, sconce*?

Use the rating scale below. Write out your definitions and compare them to the suggestions at the end of the chapter. Be aware that the ratings are not strictly ranked for all words. So, for instance, you may be able to give a synonym (level 5) but have problems with examples (level 4):

1   I have heard or seen the word before.
2   I know something about the meaning.

3   I can give examples of how to use the word, e.g. sentences with the word in.

4   I can produce exemplars of the word, e.g. given *house*, I can produce *bungalow*, *cottage*, *manor*, *villa* etc. However, this is rarely possible with very specific words (like *raspberry*).

5   I can explain the meaning (or different meanings) of the word and/or provide synonyms.

6   I can give a theoretical definition of the word – including superior concept and defining features.

sure I know what it means" – to being able to explain the word's meaning in-depth and giving typical examples of its uses.

Vocabulary knowledge is not all or none, i.e. there are different degrees of knowledge of the meaning(s) of a word. The amount and detail of knowledge of words is often referred to as *depth* of vocabulary knowledge. Depth of vocabulary knowledge also includes the relations and associations between individual words and concepts. For example, knowledge of decompression sickness might include the information that it is something scuba divers might be prone to. More "in-depth" knowledge might include the fact that it typically occurs following a rapid ascent following a long and/or deep dive. Even deeper knowledge would be that decompression illness occurs because the nitrogen bubbles that are absorbed into the diver's bodily tissues under pressure (at depth) can cause pains, and even fatalities, if they expand too quickly during a rapid ascent because they might enter the bloodstream and block blood vessels.

Recent work has demonstrated that comprehension is particularly dependent on vocabulary knowledge at relatively *deep* levels (i.e. from level 4 and below in Activity 5.2). By comparison, it is less beneficial to comprehension to know lots of words but only at more superficial levels (Ouellette, 2006; Tannenbaum, Torgesen, & Wagner, 2006).

There are several reasons why readers need a relatively deep understanding of words. First, when a text describes concepts that already have names such as *dugong* or *table*, it is, of course, easier for the reader to understand the text the more s/he knows about the key words. The chances are that the reader can already activate a rich mental model at the first encounter of the key word (e.g., Anderson, Stevens, Shifrin, & Osborn, 1978). For instance, if a reader sees the text *"The fisherman looked at his watch"*, the mental model of the watch is probably a sturdy and waterproof wristwatch or pocketwatch, not just any abstract watch. An additional problem is that a reader might know the meaning of a word, but might fail to activate and use that knowledge in the process of comprehension. For instance, children may possess relevant knowledge, but not necessarily activate it and use it to make inferences during comprehension (Cain & Oakhill, 1999; Cain, Oakhill, Barnes, & Bryant, 2001).

Second, when words are strung together, the links between their meanings are usually based on only *some aspects* of the full meanings of the words. This is easily seen with words that have many potential meanings, e.g. *table*, but only one meaning in a particular context, e.g. *the table of contents*. It is much more likely that the reader understands the word in the context if the reader already knows the particular meaning or potential meaning. However, a rich vocabulary knowledge is certainly also important for understanding the combined meanings of different words – both via local cohesion inferences and global coherence inferences. For example: *"She opened the door and noticed that the window was open."* To make sense of this very short text, the reader has to connect *door* and *window*. This may seem trivial, but a significant amount of knowledge is involved: both door and window are parts of a room or a building, so opening a door into a room may bring the window into view (Figure 5.1).

Reading comprehension occurs in real time, so fast and accurate access to word meanings (and, indeed, other sorts of knowledge) is crucial. The reader must activate word meanings within a fraction of a second in order to connect possible aspects of the word meanings into a mental model. If the activation is too slow, the word meanings will not connect before new words are encountered. So *speed of activation* is an additional requirement to the requirement of a rich vocabulary. Knowing many aspects of the meaning of many words is not enough, if it takes a long time to activate them. For example, in our recent research (see Cain & Oakhill, in press; Oakhill, Cain, McCarthy, & Nightingale, 2012) we have been exploring different aspects of children's vocabulary knowledge and their relation comprehension skill. We looked at what children knew about words at deeper levels. In addition we also investigated the children's facility of access to the word meanings at the deeper levels. We did this by asking the children to produce synonyms or hypernyms, e.g. "rain is a sort of what?" (answer: weather), and by asking them to do speeded synonym and hypernym judgements on word pairs. So, for example, they had to judge as quickly as possible whether the first item was a "type of" the second, e.g. bread–vegetable, fox–animal. We found that children's vocabulary knowledge at deep levels, and in particular the speed with which that knowledge could be accessed, was closely related to comprehension skill even when word reading ability and general speed of responding were taken into account.

Measures of vocabulary

Broadly speaking, a person's vocabulary is the total number words that the person knows and how much he or she knows about them. It is practically impossible to measure a

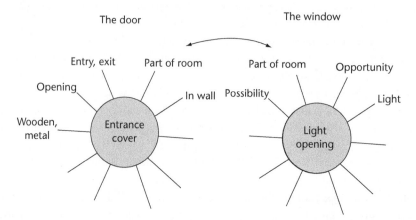

FIGURE 5.1 Links between words can be based on shared aspects of word meanings. For example, "She opened the door and noticed that the window was open." To understand this micro-text, a link between the vocabulary items *door* and *window* is essential.

person's vocabulary directly because there are hundreds of thousands of words that s/he might know. So measures (or tests) of vocabulary are restricted to word samples. In practice, a vocabulary test is also restricted to just one level of word knowledge (see Activity 5.2). So some tests only require fairly superficial word knowledge, while others are more demanding and require, for example, definitions of the words in the sample.

Tests of vocabulary knowledge at *shallow levels* are also known as tests of vocabulary *breadth*. This term can be misleading because *all* published tests of vocabulary are tests of the number of words that a person knows, i.e. the breadth of his or her vocabulary. In any case, vocabulary tests at shallow levels typically require simple recognition or production of single words. A common format is the one used in the *British Picture Vocabulary Scale* (BPVS: Dunn, Dunn, Whetton, & Pintilie, 1992), in which the person listens to a word and is asked to point to the correct picture out of a selection of four pictures. The BPVS is only a moderate predictor of reading comprehension development in young readers (Nation, Cocksey, Taylor, & Bishop, 2010; Oakhill & Cain, 2012). Another type of breadth measure requires selection of the right synonym for a spoken or written word. For example: "What is the best definition of *homogeneous*: afraid, political, uniform, guilty?"

Tests of vocabulary knowledge at *deeper levels* are also known as tests of vocabulary *depth*. Again, this can be a misleading terminology, because these tests do measure the size (or breadth) of the vocabulary at relatively deep levels. Typical tests of vocabulary at deeper levels are tasks that require production of word definitions, e.g. level 5 in Activity 5.2, or (rapid) production of exemplars of a category, e.g. level 4 in Activity 5.2. Such tasks are strongly correlated with reading comprehension (Ouellette, 2006; Tannenbaum et al., 2006).

Tests of the speed of *vocabulary activation* are not (yet) commonly available. Some examples from recent research include category judgement – for example, is *a chair* a sort of *furniture*? – and measures of vocabulary fluency (see below).

Vocabulary development

Very young children's learning of new vocabulary already involves inference making (see Chapter 4) because very young children cannot be taught word definitions. So, they typically have things labelled for them, and have to extract and refine meanings themselves by working out what the crucial features are. Indeed, they might focus on salient, but not necessarily definitional features. For example, a child might learn the word *moon* and apply it appropriately to refer to the moon, or pictures of the moon, but might also overextend to cakes, round cards, round marks on a window, the letter O, and broadly, anything round. Similarly, *horse* might be learnt and overextended to pigs, cows, and, indeed, all four-legged animals.

Receptive vocabulary (number of spoken words understood) develops earlier than productive vocabulary (number of words produced), as evidenced by the fact that young children can understand words and short phrases (e.g. "give me the ball") before they can utter even a single word.

Vocabulary is an example of what Paris (2005) calls an unconstrained skill, that is, it is learned over a long time, and the number of things to be learned is practically infinite. The learning of new vocabulary items continues throughout adult life and older adults (in their 60s) typically have more extensive vocabularies than younger adults. Thus, vocabulary knowledge can influence reading comprehension not only in the early stages of reading development, but throughout a reader's life. In particular, depth of knowledge about words, and the associations between word meanings, will continue to be developed and refined. In contrast, constrained skills, such as letter knowledge, are learned quickly and one can have complete knowledge (i.e. know all the letters in a specific alphabet). Children typically know all the letters in the alphabet before they start learning to read (though this is not a prerequisite).

Children acquire new vocabulary at an astonishing rate. Estimates of a typical adult's vocabulary put it at around 50,000 words. Young children acquire several new words per day. Children from different backgrounds start school with very different-sized vocabularies. So, those with smaller vocabularies when they start to read will already be at a disadvantage when it comes to reading comprehension, and their poorer vocabularies cannot be easily compensated for.

One source of this impressive gain in vocabulary knowledge is access to the constituent units of meaning (morphemes) in words. For instance, a young child may readily understand relatively infrequent words like *handball* and *handrail* because the child already knows the words *hand*, *ball*, and *rail*. The child also needs a basic understanding of the conventions for compound formation: the core of the meaning of the compound word is the last morpheme, e.g. *ball* in *handball*. If the child already knows other ball words and games, such as football or basketball, then s/he can form compound words by analogy. By application of morphological knowledge to words and their morphemes, children may acquire many complex words almost as if by magic: *uncommon* from *un-* and *common*, *strangely* from *strange* and *-ly* (e.g. Sparks & Deacon, 2013; Tong, Deacon, Kirby, Cain, & Parrila, 2011), though, of course, some letter strings look like morphemes but are not, e.g. *carpet* does not comprise the morphemes *car* and *pet*.

Reading experience makes the two-way street wider (a dual carriageway?)

Once children start reading, most new vocabulary is learned through reading, not from being taught (Cunningham, 2005). So, vocabulary supports reading comprehension, and reading (with good comprehension) supports vocabulary development, meaning that there is reciprocity between the development of these competencies. Indeed, a study by Seigneuric and Ehrlich (2005) showed just such a pattern. They found that vocabulary skills in 7- and 8-year-olds were related to reading comprehension later, at age 9, a finding consistent with other studies that show that vocabulary strongly predicts reading comprehension in the early years of school (Bast & Reitsma, 1998; de Jong & van der Leij, 2002). But they also found that early reading comprehension was a good predictor of vocabulary in the two older age groups. As Stanovich (1986) has argued, if the development of vocabulary knowledge substantially facilitates reading comprehension, and if reading itself is a major mechanism in improvement of vocabulary knowledge, then reading should continue to drive further vocabulary development.

The mediating variable seems to be amount of reading experience, so that those who have good comprehension (or good vocabulary) and, thus, read more, go on to improve their vocabulary (or comprehension). Indeed, there are enormous differences in the amount of reading that children do voluntarily. Nagy and Anderson (1984) estimated that in the middle grades the average children might read 100,000 words a year while the motivated children might read 1,000,000 words. Really voracious readers might read 10 million or even up to 50 million words in a year. Thus, the enormous individual differences between readers will lead to very substantial differences in vocabulary and comprehension in later years. Stanovich (1986) has termed this effect the "Matthew effect", because it encapsulates the idea that the "rich get richer". More generally, the idea of Matthew effects comes from the finding that children who have early advantageous educational experiences are able to take advantage of new educational experiences more effectively. Walberg, Strykowski, Rovai, and Hung (1984) argued that facilitating relations, like the one between vocabulary and reading, may be the source of large individual differences in educational achievement.

The reciprocal relation between vocabulary development and reading comprehension is also evidenced by work from even younger children. A study on generating inferences from picture books found that this skill when children were aged 4 years predicted their vocabulary knowledge 1 year later, which predicted their listening comprehension (Lepola, Lynch, Laakkonen, Silvén, & Niemi, 2012). This finding speaks to the need to foster inference skills, not only because of their importance for understanding extended text, but also for their importance in developing vocabulary knowledge.

As mentioned earlier, vocabulary knowledge in both children and adults is strongly associated with reading comprehension (Carroll, 1993), but the relation between them is not static throughout development. The importance of vocabulary knowledge to reading comprehension has been shown to increase between about 7 and 10 years (Protopapas, Sideridis, Mouzaki, & Simos, 2007), probably because, as children become more skilled and fluent word decoders, vocabulary becomes more important as a predictor of comprehension skill. Another plausible reason for the increasing contribution of vocabulary knowledge might be that, as children get older, the books they need to read and understand have more challenging vocabulary (beginning reading books are typically written with a restricted word set), though, as we discuss below, it is not simply "knowing" the words that is important for comprehension, but having rich networks of associations between word meanings.

The development of reading comprehension thus entails the addition of words to a reader's lexicon, as well as the refinement and consolidation of the meanings of known words. As explained above, readers will also gradually learn more about words' meanings and establish and strengthen the associations between words (their depth of knowledge).

Vocabulary difficulties

As would be expected, some poor comprehenders have weak vocabulary knowledge. However, as mentioned above, the links between vocabulary knowledge and reading comprehension are complex, reciprocal, and develop over time. So it is not surprising that there can be several different relations between vocabulary difficulties and reading comprehension difficulties. Four different links between weak vocabulary knowledge and comprehension problems can be discerned:

First, poor comprehension limits vocabulary growth. Some of our own data demonstrates that children with specific reading comprehension difficulties have slower rates of vocabulary growth than same-age peers with good reading comprehension (Cain & Oakhill, 2011).

Second, vocabulary knowledge at *shallow levels* (vocabulary breadth, see above) is *not* clearly causally linked to poor comprehension. Children identified as poor comprehenders do not typically have poor receptive vocabulary: they can perform within the normal range on measures of vocabulary at relatively *shallow levels* (vocabulary breadth), but still have problems with comprehension. These children have problems with other aspects of vocabulary or with other components of reading comprehension (Cain, Oakhill, & Lemmon, 2004).

Third, vocabulary at *deeper levels* (vocabulary depth, see above) is likely to be causally linked to poor comprehension. The reasons were presented in the above section on "Vocabulary: breadth, depth, and access".

Fourth, poor comprehenders also appear to perform relatively poorly on measures of *activation of word meanings and related words*, for example on vocabulary fluency tasks. Poor comprehenders generate fewer category instances than good comprehenders (e.g. name as many kinds of *birds* as you can). The poor comprehenders' problem is specific to tasks requiring access to word *meanings*, because they are good at a similar task that requires them to generate rhyming words (name as many words that rhyme with *bird* as you can) (Nation & Snowling, 1998). But there is probably quite a lot of variability within poor comprehenders.

There is also evidence that good comprehenders are more likely than poor comprehenders to activate meaning-related words automatically. Try Activity 5.3.

Activity 5.3 Which words do you activate?

• Read the following list of words *once*, slowly, while you try to memorise them:

> bed, rest, tired, dream, wake, snooze, blanket, doze, slumber, snore, nap, peace, yawn, drowsy, door, glass, pane, shade, ledge, sill, house, open, curtain, frame, view, breeze, sash, screen, shutter

• Now go to the end of the chapter and take the memory test for this Activity 5.3, before reading on.

We used a memory task (like the one in Activity 5.3) to assess good and poor comprehenders' gist memory for word lists (Weekes, Hamilton, Oakhill, & Holliday, 2008). The children were asked to try to remember the lists, and were then asked if certain words had occurred in the list, some of which they had heard, and some not. Of particular interest were the false recollections – the good comprehenders were *more* likely to make an interesting error: they often claimed that they had heard a "theme word" which was not presented, but which captured the gist of the word list (for the above lists the theme words were *sleep* and *window*). So if you falsely thought that you had seen those gist words in the lists, it may be because you are a good comprehender. Good comprehenders automatically activate words that are related in meaning to those they read.

To summarise, the available evidence suggests that the link *from* vocabulary *to* comprehension has at least three potential bases: (1) detailed knowledge of a word's meaning; (2) activation of the relevant aspects of a word's meaning (and meaning-related words); and (3) use of that information to support comprehension. Thus, it may be that the facility of access to word meanings (as measured by the speed with which meanings can be retrieved) and use of that activated knowledge, rather than knowledge of these meanings in itself, is critical for text comprehension.

Vocabulary knowledge beyond single words

Another type of vocabulary knowledge, though not at the word level, is knowledge of fixed expressions. These might include common sayings and idioms, which behave like multiword lexical items. Most idioms have a clear literal meaning, and so whether the intended meaning is literal or figurative depends on the context. In a sense, idioms behave rather like ambiguous words, in that the intended meaning has to be inferred from the context. For example, the expression "to be in the same boat" has a literal meaning in the passage *"during the trip on the lake, Steve met John since they were in the same boat"*, whereas the same expression has a figurative meaning in the passage *"Stephen and John lost their jobs last summer. They became true friends since they were in the same boat."*

Activity 5.4 Figure out the idioms

- Try to explain the meaning of the following idioms from European languages other than English:
  - to shoot sparrows with cannons
  - to pet the horse first.
- Here are the idioms in context. Now try to explain what they mean.

    Tommy was terribly upset one day when he saw a dead woodlouse in the lounge. He suggested to his mother that they should take up the floorboards because the woodlouse must have come in from under the floor. His mother tried to calm him down and said that they should not shoot sparrows with cannons.

    Selma's youngest daughter had moved to Scotland to go into bicycle sales. The day after she moved, Selma met with an estate agent and signed a binding offer to buy a luxury flat in the city centre. Only later, when her old house proved impossible to sell, did she realise that she had petted the horse first.

As is the case with vocabulary learning, children differ in their ability to work out the figurative meaning of idioms in context. Interesting work has been done on idioms that are unfamiliar because they do not come from the child's native language. In such cases, the child must combine a semantic analysis of the phrase with inferences of a likely meaning using the context. This is a good way to control for familiarity when investigating how context affects idiom interpretation. Cain, Oakhill, and Lemmon (2005) found that good comprehenders were better at explaining the meanings of both real (English) and novel (translations of European) idioms when they when they were presented in supportive contexts as opposed to being presented in isolation (as in Activity 5.4). The poorer comprehenders were not helped by context to nearly the same extent as were the better comprehenders (Cain et al., 2005; Cain & Towse, 2008; Levorato, Nesi, & Cacciari, 2004). These findings have also been extended to differences between age groups (Cain, Towse, & Knight, 2009): older children (9- to 10-year-olds) are better at using context to interpret novel idioms than are younger ones (7- to 8-year-olds).

Furthermore, the relation between text comprehension and ability to understand idioms seems to be more than a simple relation between different measures of language skill: a study that followed up the ability of 6-year-old children found that their skill in understanding idioms was more strongly related to their text comprehension skill 8 months later than were other linguistic abilities such as syntax (Levorato, Roch, & Nesi, 2007).

Teaching vocabulary

There is evidence that substituting easier vocabulary words for harder words and instruction in the meaning of more difficult words can improve comprehension (Kameenui, Carnine, & Freschi, 1982). However, it cannot be a long-term strategy to adapt texts for children with poor vocabularies: first of all, logistically, this is not a realistic possibility and second, it is important that children learn to infer meanings from context so that they increase their vocabulary and not just have texts simplified to the level of their existing vocabulary.

Although quite a lot is known about the importance of vocabulary to success in reading, there is relatively little empirical research on the best methods, or combinations of methods, of vocabulary instruction. Not surprisingly, it is not possible to teach children vocabulary in ways that will dramatically expand and deepen their vocabulary. The immediate results of vocabulary training are moderate, and the transfer effects to reading comprehension are even smaller. They have only shown up in a small number of studies (National Reading Panel (NRP), 2000). However, there are promising ways in which the interplay between vocabulary knowledge and reading comprehension may be improved.

Two different purposes of teaching vocabulary can be distinguished. The most obvious is simply to help children learn the meanings of *specific* words. The other is to help children become better at *figuring out meanings of new* words through independent reading. Both purposes help to support the development of reading comprehension. The ways of teaching for these purposes are rather different, so they will be described in turn in this section.

Teaching specific words. Even key words are frequently left unexplained in school texts. Authors take word knowledge for granted even though many words may be unfamiliar to children. In such cases, it can be helpful to explain key words and to link them to topic knowledge *before* the children read the text. When key words are known, it is much easier to use them to build mental models of the content of the text. For instance, for fifth-grade students, teaching relevant vocabulary has an effect on learning of and memory for a social studies text (Carney, Anderson, Blackburn, & Blessing, 1984), and Medo and Ryder (1993) found that vocabulary instruction helped eighth-grade students to make causal connections in an informational text, and that this method was beneficial for both average and high-ability students.

In addition to key words, other words may also be targeted for direct teaching. These are words that children are likely to encounter frequently in texts as they enter higher grade levels, words such as *essential, decent, unwarranted, inevitably, sobering* ("tier two words" in the US; Beck, McKeown, & Kucan, 2005). They are neither the most frequent and early-acquired words ("tier one") nor infrequent, topic-specific words ("tier three"). Since words are learned in approximately the same order no matter whether they are learned at the age of 7 or 10, tier two words are the ones that are either just included or about to be included in the child's vocabulary (Biemiller, 2005). As such, they are among the most useful words that could be selected for teaching.

There are numerous ways to teach vocabulary, and the research base is not strong enough to form strong recommendations about which is best (NRP, 2000). Some trends are worth mentioning though:

As would be expected given the links between vocabulary and reading comprehension, the successful teaching of vocabulary has to be aimed at deeper levels of vocabulary knowledge. This means that children should not just learn word definitions, but also how unfamiliar words relate to other words. So, for example, it is not enough to learn that a "borzoi" is a name of a particular animal. It is much more efficient to know that a borzoi is a type of dog, in which ways it is a typical dog, and how it differs from most other dogs. In this way, borzoi will be linked to many other words and concepts in a "semantic network" (or meaning network).

In practice, this means that vocabulary teaching should take place in a rich context (Beck, Perfetti, & McKeown, 1982; NRP, 2000) preferably in long-lasting work on important themes. The formation of connections (networks) between words should be actively encouraged.

Vocabulary learning is also enhanced when children are given opportunities to detect and to use new words, e.g. during dialogues with the teacher (Coyne, McCoach, & Kapp, 2007). The teacher can support learning by asking increasingly demanding questions about new words (e.g., Blewitt, Rump, Shealy, & Cook, 2009).

Repetitions of new vocabulary items are also supportive to learning as already pointed out in the influential survey of training studies by Stahl and Fairbanks (1986). This means that pre-reading activities with key words should be followed up by activities on what has been learned about these words during reading, and follow-up activities on later occasions. For younger children, simple re-reading of storybooks will provide them with important opportunities to rehearse the meaning of new words (Biemiller & Boote, 2006).

Teaching children to acquire new vocabulary. Even though it may be possible for children to learn 10 new words a week through a well-structured vocabulary programme (Biemiller, 2005), such a programme would help children to acquire only about 400 new words a year. This would still only be a small fraction of the words that children typically acquire in a year. A further complication is that it would be difficult for the teacher to predict which key content words the children would need to know in the longer run. This is why some more recent programmes (see below) teach children word knowledge and inference making abilities that may help them acquire new word knowledge during independent reading.

There are two common ways to help children improve incidental learning of vocabulary. They are not mutually exclusive; rather, they may supplement each other. One way is to instruct children in ways to derive meanings from context. Children can be taught to search the context for clues about the unknown word's category ("what sort of thing is it?"), for defining characteristics ("how can you describe it?"), and for likes and opposites ("do you know of something similar or the opposite?"). For instance, Tomesen and Aarnoutse (1998) found that such direct instruction was helpful in improving the text comprehension of both poor and average readers. However, the skills did not transfer to the children's reading comprehension more generally.

Another way is to teach word knowledge through morphology, that is, through knowledge of the smallest significant units of words: prefixes, roots, suffixes, inflections, e.g. *mis/read/ing/s* (see Bowers & Kirby, 2010). The same root morphemes occur in several different words, e.g. the root *read* is part of *reads, reader, unread, reading* etc., and derivations and inflections apply to whole classes of words. So learning a morpheme in one word is potentially beneficial for recognising and understanding many new words in which the morpheme occurs. In a review of 22 studies, Bowers, Kirby, and Deacon (2010) found that teaching morphology to children had significant effects on the development of both vocabulary and reading comprehension. Such effects were enhanced if teaching did not just focus on the analysis of single words but was combined with comprehension instruction.

Generally, successful training programmes appear to explicitly emphasise the interrelations between the orthographic, phonological, morphological, semantic, and syntactic aspects of reading. The basic premise is that the more one knows about a word (i.e. its phonemes, orthographic patterns, semantic meanings, syntactic uses, and morphological roots and affixes), the more efficiently the word is decoded, retrieved, and comprehended. Such a programme, called RAVE-O (Barzillai, Morris, Lovett, & Wolf, 2010), which focuses on training meaning in the context of the other linguistic properties of the word to be learnt, has been shown to improve second- and third-grade struggling poor readers' knowledge. This training was effective, not only for the multiple meanings of the words taught within the programme, but also improved the children's knowledge of the meanings of words not taught within the programme. Importantly, these gains were maintained 1 year later.

Summary

Knowing the meanings of words is obviously crucial for reading comprehension, but the link between vocabulary and reading flows in both directions. Once children learn to read fairly independently, they learn new vocabulary items through reading, and not through direct teaching of meanings. Thus, the amount of reading that children do in the early school years will be a crucial determinant of their vocabulary development. "Having a good vocabulary" has different aspects, which are both important for reading comprehension. First, it can mean knowing the meanings of a large number of words, which is termed vocabulary breadth, and is typically assessed by tasks of rather superficial knowledge, such as picking a picture that represents a spoken word, or choosing a synonym. Second, it can refer to vocabulary depth – that is, knowing a lot about the meaning of the word, and how its meaning is related to that of other known words. Depth of vocabulary understanding has been shown to be more strongly related to reading comprehension skill than has vocabulary breadth, probably because depth of understanding is a measure of the richness and interconnectedness of a reader's meaning networks, which are crucial in supporting important comprehension skills like making inferences.

Vocabulary should be taught both directly, especially in the case of key words and terms that are likely to be unknown to readers (explicit definitions, e.g. pre-teaching of core vocabulary before reading a text), and indirectly (to enhance the reader's ability to infer and refine word meanings from a text). Therefore, training to improve word knowledge should not be only about teaching more words. As Nagy and Herman (1987) remarked, "the size of the task is such that just teaching more words cannot be seen as the answer". Thus, the word meanings that are selected for direct teaching should be those that the child needs at that stage: those words that are important in understanding what they need to read, and are important for learning more words. Moreover, children need to be encouraged to try to work out the meanings of unknown words for themselves, to look up words (it has never been easier), and to refine the meanings of words they already know to some extent, so that they learn to learn vocabulary for themselves (Stahl & Fairbanks, 1986).

Glossary

Morphology: The study and description of the meaning components of words. A morpheme is the smallest linguistic unit (part of a word) that has meaning. So, a word can consist of a single morpheme: *happy* (the root morpheme) and its meaning can be changed by adding morphemes: *un+happy*, *happi+ness*, etc., to create derived words. A morphemic analysis can help with the derivation of complex, multi-morphemic words, e.g. *antidisestablishmentarianism*. Plural suffixes are also morphemes (*dog+s*), though in this case the base meaning of the word does not change.

Orthography: An orthography is a writing system (script) for a particular language. It includes rules of spelling.

Vocabulary access: How easily words are retrieved, either produced (e.g. in a picture naming task) or identified (e.g. during reading).

Vocabulary breadth: The number of words in the vocabulary.

Vocabulary depth: How much is known about the meaning of words, and how they relate to each other.

Suggested answers to activities

Activity 5.1 The two-way street between vocabulary and comprehension

- You should have been able to glean some information about the dugong and where its natural habitat is. For instance, it is a sea animal that does not have a dorsal fin, but has paddle-like forearms and a dolphin-like tail, and it eats sea grass.
- There may be words in the text whose meaning you do not know, e.g. *sirenian*, *fusiform*, and *benthic*. The dugong is probably related to the manatee, so it would be useful to know what a manatee is. In contrast, the special *benthic* type of sea grass that it lives on is probably not the most important bit of information.

Activity 5.2 How deep is your knowledge of these words?

- *Table:* (noun) a table is a kind of furniture. It has a flat and usually level surface that is supported by typically one leg (café table), three legs (coffee table), or four legs (dining or work table). It is used to support objects during activities where the objects are in use such as dining and working. Table has multiple other meanings, as in e.g. *time table* and *table of contents*.
- *Maroon:* a) (verb) to abandon or isolate with little hope of ready rescue or escape, b) (noun) a dark reddish brown to dark purplish red.
- *Auspices:* (noun) support or protection, typically used in the phrase "under the auspices of…".
- *Quator:* sorry, this is not a word in English (*equator* is).
- *Sconce:* a) (noun) a decorative wall bracket for holding candles or lights, b) (noun) small defensive earthwork or fort.

Activity 5.3 Which words do you activate?

- Which of the following words were in the word lists? Write them down!

  snore, towel, empty, frame, dream, bottle, sleep, pane, brush, rest, window, ledge

OK, go back to the activity and see how well you did.

Activity 5.4 Figure out the idioms

- *To shoot sparrows with cannons* means "to use excessive means to fulfil an objective".
- *To pet the horse first* means "to rush (into) something leads to mistakes".

6

SENTENCES AND THEIR CONNECTIONS

"Charlotte Rampling will be 60 next year and is only too happy to admit it: …'I'm a grandmother three times over and very proud of it,' she said. 'Two of them live in London and one in Paris. It's absolutely lovely to be able to cuddle them as babies'."

From The Sunday Times, 15 May 2005

The odd thing about the short text above is that the pronoun *them* in the final and penultimate sentences of the quotation does not seem to relate directly to any entities previously mentioned in the text. That is because pronouns usually have what are termed "antecedents" (i.e. things going before) – other words or phrases, usually in the preceding text – from which they take their meaning. In the above text there is no explicit antecedent for the word *them* – it has to be inferred – the grandchildren that come by virtue of being a grandmother.

Pronouns are one type of cohesive tie that can be used to bind sentences. Another, that we consider in this chapter, is the connective – words such as *before* and *because* that can signal how the meanings of sentences are related, for example in time or the causal relation. Pronouns, and other anaphors, and connectives are typically understood effortlessly when we read, at least when we are reading well-written texts. For example, it is rare that we, as skilled language users, need to stop and think about what a pronoun means.

The purposes of this chapter are:

- to provide an overview of the ties that bind clauses and sentences together: various cohesive ties, such as co-reference and conjunction,
- to highlight the challenges that syntax and sentence ties pose to the developing reader and to readers with comprehension problems,
- to suggest ways in which proficiency with such ties may be assessed – and supported by teaching.

Understanding sentence structure

By the time children enter school, their spoken language comprehension is usually far better than their reading comprehension. That is because they have not yet acquired fluent word decoding, not because they have difficulties with the relatively simple syntax (sentence structure) of the books they encounter in school. Of course, children with Specific Language Impairment (SLI) are known to have problems with reading comprehension, and also often have difficulties with sentence understanding (Bishop, 1997; Snowling & Hulme, 2005). Some children who are poor at reading comprehension, but without a formal diagnosis of SLI, might have milder language problems (Nation & Norbury, 2005).

However, although children have quite advanced syntactic skills when they start learning to read, a good deal of syntactic development occurs during the primary school years (see e.g. Chomsky, 1969). For instance, Jessie Reid (1972) showed that children of about 7 or 8 years of age not only have trouble understanding embedded relative clauses (which, as we saw in Chapter 1, are common in written text, but rare in spoken communication) but consistently *misinterpret* them. For instance, given the sentence: *"The girl standing beside the lady was wearing a red dress"* (where *standing beside the lady* is the embedded clause), and asked: "Who was wearing a red dress?" children in this age range will consistently claim that it was "the lady". However, even though a certain level of syntactic skill will be required for comprehension to develop, syntax does not seem to be one of the main drivers of comprehension development (Oakhill & Cain, 2012). It is likely, rather, that extensive reading and familiarisation with the syntactic constructions that are found in texts will be important.

During the school years, the syntactic demands of written texts continue to increase. In secondary school it is easy to find texts that have syntactic complexities that are beyond those of everyday spoken communication. Examples are reversible passives, e.g. *"the red cat was chased by the little boy"*, and embedded relative clauses as described above, e.g. *"the cat that those of us who actually owned the house found under the sofa was not at all familiar to us"*. Such constructions are difficult to understand for many children in primary school, and in some cases the constructions continue to be obscure even for adults.

The difficulty of the constructions is, however, strongly mediated by the contents. This is easily seen in the case of passives. When there is only one sensible interpretation of who the agent and the recipient or object are, the passive construction is not so much of a problem, e.g. *"The car was washed by the young lad"* is non-reversible (because the young lad cannot be washed by the car) and simple, whereas *"The blonde was washed by the young lad"* is reversible and more difficult to understand. This means that comprehension will be intact in most cases even when the syntactic complexity is taxing the reader's abilities.

Difficulties with sentence structure: knowledge and awareness

The building blocks of text are words and sentences, so it is not surprising that children with reading comprehension difficulties have sometimes been shown to have poor syntactic knowledge (Nation, Clarke, Marshall, & Durand, 2004; Stothard & Hulme, 1992). However, other studies (which have used the same assessment of syntactic *knowledge*: the Test for the Reception of Grammar; Bishop, 1983) have not provided evidence that poor text comprehenders also have difficulties at the sentence level (Cain & Oakhill, in press; Cain, Patson, & Andrews, 2005; Yuill & Oakhill, 1991). The test of syntactic knowledge assesses understanding of spoken sentences with different structures, such as relatively simple types with three elements, e.g. "The dog stands on the table", more difficult relative constructions, e.g. "The girl that is jumping points at the man", and the most difficult centre-embedded sentences, such as "The sheep the girl looks at is running". Children are required to select one out of four pictures that matches the meaning of the spoken sentences, so it is an assessment of knowledge and comprehension of these constructions. The discrepancy in results between these different studies may have arisen because different poor comprehenders have different patterns of strengths and weaknesses, and only some have problems at the sentence level (or with particular sentence types). However, the relation between syntactic knowledge and comprehension skill is not strong, especially when considered in relation to the importance of other processes in reading comprehension (see e.g. Oakhill & Cain, 2012).

Other tasks address syntactic *awareness*, rather than knowledge. These tasks assess children's ability to consciously reflect on sentence structures, using tasks such as correction of disordered sentences (e.g. "John to school walked") and asking them to reorder them, or to detect errors in such sentences. There is clearer evidence that good and poor comprehenders differ on such tasks. For example, Gaux and Gombert (1999) found that 12-year-old poor comprehenders performed more poorly on such tasks, and Bentin, Deutsch, and Liberman (1990) and Nation and Snowling (2000) found that poor comprehenders make more errors on tasks of syntactic awareness than do good comprehenders. Children with poor text comprehension might do more poorly on these syntactic awareness tasks because such tasks require metacognitive monitoring, and there is substantial evidence that poor comprehenders lack this ability more generally (see Chapter 8).

One possible explanation that has been proposed for the link between syntactic skills and reading comprehension is that they are related by phonological processing skills, which support working memory (see later in this chapter). According to Shankweiler and his colleagues (see Shankweiler, 1989, for a review), comprehension difficulties can arise when children are unable to set up or sustain a phonological representation of verbal information. As a result, they have problems processing information in verbal working memory, which would adversely affect their ability to understand syntactically complex constructions (see e.g. Smith, Macaruso, Shankweiler, & Crain, 1989).

In summary, successful reading experiences will help children become familiar with the specific and complex syntactical structures of written language. It is, of course, important that the teacher is aware that children may find some syntactic constructions difficult, or might even misunderstand them systematically, but it is probably better to expose children to well-written text, rather than to explicitly try to teach them more complex syntactic constructions.

Cohesive ties aid comprehension

Understanding of sentences that have particular syntactic structures, such as passives and relative clauses, is clearly important for good reading comprehension, as discussed. Although sentences with these structures may be easier to understand when embedded in a supportive context, they are to a large extent understood in isolation. However, as discussed in Chapter 1 of this book, successful comprehenders integrate the meanings of successive clauses and sentences in a text as they construct a memory-based representation of the text's meaning. These integration processes can be guided by linguistic knowledge; in particular anaphors and connectives. These are the topic of this section.

Anaphors. An anaphor takes its meaning from another part of the text (its antecedent). Common anaphors include pronouns, such as *it, he, she,* or *they,* and verb phrase ellipsis, as in the sentence: *"She won't have another slice of cake, but he will [have another slice of cake]."* Because the interpretation of a pronoun or an ellipsis is dependent on its antecedent, resolution of anaphors results in the integration of the meanings of different clauses and sentences. An example of this linkage is provided by the following sentence pair: *"Molly was tired. She went to bed."* If the comprehender successfully resolves the pronoun *she* to refer back to the character Molly, a link between the two clauses has been established.

Pronouns carry almost no intrinsic meaning, and need to take their meaning from their antecedents. In English the gender (*she* vs. *he*), number (singular or plural, e.g. *she* vs. *they*), case (subjective, e.g. *I, she, he, it* vs. objective, e.g. *me, you, him, whomever* vs. possessive, e.g. *his, its, theirs*), and animacy (*she* vs. *it*) of the pronoun are marked, which can cue the pronoun's antecedent. Thus, *he* and *she* are pronouns that refer to male and female characters, respectively. When the pronoun *he* is used in a text with two male protagonists there is no gender cue to aid the reader and additional inferential processing will be required to identify the correct antecedent. For the sentence, *"Steven gave his umbrella to Jack in the park because he wanted to keep dry"*, the comprehender must infer that the likely recipient of the umbrella is the person who wants to keep dry (Oakhill & Yuill, 1986). In contrast, when one protagonist is male and the other female, the gender information can be used to identify the antecedent without the need for additional inferential processing.

Another frequent use of anaphors occurs when a word or words are omitted to avoid repetition – so called *ellipses*. These are very frequent in both written and spoken communication, and avoid repetition. For example, *"John went to the pub on Friday evening. Fred did too."* In this case, *did too*, means *went to the pub too*, and the use of ellipsis saves repeating the whole phrase.

Activity 6.1 Pronoun resolution

- What does each of the pronouns refer to in these examples?
- How did you know?
  - Peter lent his car to Paul because *he* had missed the last train.
  - Peter lent his car to David because *he* had a broken ankle.
  - Nicki pulled the dagger from the corpse. *It* had a silver handle. *It* was probably that of a burglar.
  - Eve asked the surgeon if *she* knew which finger was causing trouble.

Lexical cohesion. Another kind of anaphoric link is created by the use of definite nouns (<u>the</u> *train*, <u>the</u> *woman*). For instance, a link is formed from *the woman* back to *a woman* in the following pair of sentences: *"A young woman was waiting patiently in her car. The woman was looking forward to seeing Caroline."* The use of a definite noun (*the woman*) indicates that the second sentence is about a particular woman, most likely someone who has been mentioned before. So the reader may carry over all the information about the woman from the previous sentences. The use of such a definite reference is similar to using a personal pronoun, except that the referent (*the woman*) is far better specified. The use of definite forms like <u>*the*</u> *woman* presupposes that the reader already knows which woman is referred to.

Lexical cohesion can take many other forms apart from the repetition of a noun. Some common possibilities are:

- Whole and part, e.g. *they took out <u>some picnic supplies</u>. <u>The cider</u> was warm.*
- Item and container, e.g. *the boy asked for <u>some orange juice</u>. His sister handed him <u>the bottle</u>.*
- Item and broader category (hypernym), e.g. *They were terribly thirsty and ordered <u>two large lagers</u>. Luckily, <u>the drinks</u> were served immediately.*
- Synonyms, e.g. *Glenn had piles of <u>jumpers</u> in a chest of drawers. On Sundays he always chose <u>the</u> blue stripy <u>pullover</u>.*

Writers often maintain a high degree of coherence by linking words into a limited number of semantic networks. Thus, establishing lexical cohesion is not necessarily effortful for readers when the text is considerate. Try to find the relations between the lexical items in the text in Activity 6.2.

Activity 6.2 Lexical links

- Find the relations between the content words in the text below.
- Is it possible to organise the linked up words into just two semantic networks?

> Most of her spare time Hanna devoted to different kinds of exercise. She particularly favoured the bike rides she would do both in the evening and at the weekend. Her new racing bike had not been cheap, but she even enjoyed riding it into town during her lunch hour.

Connectives. Connectives are words and phrases that signal the logical relations between clauses and sentences. The relations can be temporal relations between events (e.g. *before, after, a little later, during*), the direction of causality (e.g. *because, so, in consequence*), contrastive relations (e.g. *but, although, on the other hand*), and continuity (e.g. *and, also, in addition to*). These different functions are detailed in Table 6.1. The four groups of relation correspond to the four types of conjunction (following Halliday & Hasan, 1976). Connectives may be particularly useful aids to comprehension because they signal not only that two pieces of information are related, but also how they are related. Take the example: *"Chris sprained his ankle before he played football."* The presence of a temporal connective can direct the reader to the correct order of events and their interpretation: Chris was already injured before he took part in the football match. In this way, connectives may help readers to integrate sentences.

Connectives help to make a text cohesive by directing the reader to the ways in which information in different clauses and sentences is related. They can also invite the reader

TABLE 6.1 Connectives grouped by logical function

Function	Meaning and examples
Temporal	Before: *earlier, previously*... Later: *afterwards, subsequently*... Simultaneously: *during, while, at the same time*...
Causal	Cause/effect relation: *because, consequently, so, for this reason*...
Contrast	Opposites: *conversely, on the other hand*... Alternatives: *alternatively, instead*...
Continuity	Additive: *secondly, furthermore, in addition*...

to engage in inference making and constructive processing. Compare these three sentences:

> *June left the barbecue early <u>just before</u> Bill arrived.*
> *June left the barbecue early <u>after</u> Bill arrived.*
> *June left the barbecue early <u>at the very moment</u> Bill arrived.*

The relation between June and Bill appears to be going downhill under the influence of the temporal connectives. In the first sentence, the reader may or may not infer that June left early because she did not like Bill, and she did not wish to meet him. It could also be the case that the arrival of Bill is just the writer's way of marking the time, in which case June might not even know Bill. The second sentence may imply that June left the barbecue early *because* of Bill – whether she already knew him or not. The third sentence makes the relationship between June and Bill even more chilly. The point is that what the reader can determine about the relationship is all in the temporal connective – and depends on the reader's accurate knowledge of different connectives and his or her ability to draw inferences.

You can try more examples, including some difficult ones, in Activity 6.3.

Activity 6.3 The power of connectives

- What is the relationship between John and Helen like in each of these examples?
- How did you reason?
  1 *John was late <u>because</u> he was going to Helen's place.*
  2 *John was late <u>although</u> he was going to Helen's place.*
  3 *John was late <u>so</u> he was going to Helen's place.*
  4 *John was late <u>or</u> he was going to Helen's place.*

Assessment of knowledge of different cohesive devices

Pronouns and other anaphors. Children's understanding of pronouns is typically assessed by asking them questions about who did what. For the sentence *"Jack gave a book* *to Jill as a birthday present, because she loved reading"*, a simple question to tap understanding is: "Who loved reading?"

Another type of task, which can be used with children as young as 2 years old, is to ask the child to act out a statement or instruction using a puppet. The child is told to do what the puppet (e.g. *Snoopy*) says. So, if the child's name were *Sarah*, the instruction might be: *Snoopy says that Sarah should point to him* (to perform correctly the child, Sarah, should point to Snoopy) (Chien & Wexler, 1990; Arnold, Brown-Schmidt, & Trueswell, 2007).

A third type of task is created by deleting pronouns from a text so the child's task is to fill them in, or to select the right one, e.g. *"Jack gave a book to Jill as a birthday present, because (he – she – it) loved reading."* Even though this is a rather common task, it is not primarily a measure of the child's ability to connect pronouns to their antecedents, because there are *no pronouns* to connect to antecedents if a choice is not provided. Instead, it is primarily a task that measures the child's ability to make *inferences* about who is doing what in the text *without* the support from a pronoun.

Connectives. One of the most frequently used methods to assess children's understanding of connectives is a cloze task, like the one described above for pronouns. Some of the connectives in a text are deleted and children are asked either to fill in the blanks or to select which from a selection best fills the blank. However, as with pronouns, this task is not primarily a measure of the understanding of connectives if options are not provided, because there are no connectives to understand. Even if options are provided, the task is mainly a measure of the child's ability to understand (or infer) the logical relations between sentences or clauses, and only then a measure of the child's knowledge of which connectives can be used.

A more explicit test of connective understanding would be to tell children about the relationships between sentences as in Activity 6.4. That way the task is focused on the knowledge of different connectives with specific meanings.

Activity 6.4 Select the connective

- Insert a connective, in place of each of the question words, to provide the most likely meaning in these examples:

   1   Paula searched for her gloves [why?] it was cold in the morning.
   2   Paula searched for her gloves [when?] leaving the house.
   3   Paula searched for her gloves [why in the world?] she knew it was warm outside.
   4   Paula searched for her gloves [what happened?] she missed the bus.

For older children, it is also possible to assess their understanding of a range of connectives that share meanings, by asking them to replace a connective in a sentence with another that does not change the meaning. For example, in most sentences *so, consequently,* and *therefore* are synonyms, e.g. *"He forgot to take his umbrella to work. (So = consequently = therefore) he got wet when it rained."*

A relatively difficult possibility is to let children explain the meanings of short texts that only differ from one another in terms of the connectives (as in Activity 6.3).

The development of knowledge and use of cohesive devices

Pronouns

Some studies have shown that even very young children can use gender cues to understand pronouns. For instance, in Chien and Wexler's (1990) study, mentioned above, they showed that even children of 2½ years of age could make use of gender marking to perform correctly in an acting-out task. Thus, they were near perfect in acting out sentences such as "Snoopy says that Sarah should point to him", making Sarah point to Snoopy. In contrast, they had a lot of difficulty with sentences where there was no gender cue, such as *Snoopy says that Adam should point to him*, erroneously making Adam point to himself, not to Snoopy. Other studies have also shown that children from 3½ to 5 years old can make use of gender cues in listening tasks where they are asked to act out what is happening in a story, with sentences such as: "Jack is having lunch with Daisy. He wants some milk", the child would then be asked to show who wants the milk (Arnold et al., 2007; Song & Fisher, 2005).

These studies indicate that, in some contexts, young children can make use of gender cues to identify the correct antecedent of a pronoun. However, pronoun understanding becomes a great deal more difficult when there is more than one possible antecedent that matches a pronoun in number and gender. For instance, in a sentence such as: "Lucy asked Daisy to help, because she...", adults will tend to choose the first-mentioned antecedent (Lucy) in the absence of any other information (Gernsbacher & Hargreaves, 1988). This is a sensible strategy to guide pronoun understanding because the first-mentioned person or entity is typically the subject of the sentence, and subjects are typically the focus of the text (what it is about). Although sensitivity to this type of information has been shown to begin to develop between the ages of 3 and 5 years (Arnold et al., 2007; Song & Fisher, 2005), this understanding of the use of the broader text context, in combination with information from pronoun gender, develops only slowly until about 10 years of age (Kail, 1976; Tyler, 1983).

Connectives. Much of the work on children's connective processing has examined the age at which they produce connectives in their speech. Connectives appear early; by around 5 years of age children produce a range of connectives that signal different types of relation between events (Kail & Weissenborn, 1991; Spooren & Sanders, 2008). There is a pattern of acquisition: connectives that express continuity and additive relations, such as *and*, appear first, followed by temporal connectives, then causal, and finally adversative or contrastive connectives (Bloom, Lahey, Hood, Lifter, & Fiess, 1980).

The early appearance of connectives in speech suggests that young readers will benefit from connectives when they are used to link clauses to create two-clause sentences or longer. However, *appropriate* use of connectives in children's speech continues to develop for several years after they first appear in children's speech. For example, when narrating a story, 4-year-olds are more likely to use "but" when another connective would be more appropriate (Peterson, 1986), and 9-year-olds frequently use "and" to demonstrate a relation without explicit mentioned of that relation (Peterson & McCabe, 1987). This means that the presence of connectives in speech is not necessarily a good indicator of how well children understand the relations expressed by these cohesive cues and, therefore, when the use of connectives in writing will guide their reading comprehension.

As noted earlier, knowledge of connectives can be assessed by paper-and-pen tasks such as a cloze task, where children (or adults) are asked to fill in the appropriate word when a connective has been deleted, or by identifying which of two clauses that are joined by a temporal connective occurred first. Improvement on such tasks continues over a long period: 10-year-olds are typically better than 8-year-olds (Cain et al., 2005) and even 12-year-olds do not achieve adult levels of performance on these tasks (Pyykkonen & Jarvikivi, 2012). Furthermore, connectives can cause particular problems for English-language learners (Crosson, Lesaux, & Martiniello, 2008). This may be because connectives do not have a one-to-one correspondence across languages: the English connective *but* can take the form *aber* and *sondern* in German. The former (*aber*) links clauses or phrases to provide contrasting information, as in: "Jane likes apples, but she also likes pears", whereas *sondern* is used to express contrasting *correcting* information and the information to be contradicted must contain a negative word, as in: "At my school we cannot learn Spanish, but we can learn German or French."

However, the cloze task does not examine whether connectives *aid* comprehension. To do that, researchers have assessed whether or not the presence of connectives leads to better understanding of a text. Certainly for adults, the presence of connectives aids their ability to make links between events in different sentences, particularly when the topic is unfamiliar so that readers cannot use their general knowledge to make links between different pieces of information (McNamara & Kintsch, 1996). Children are sensitive to meaning signalled by connectives, but they are not as sensitive as adults. For example, when asked to judge whether sentences make sense or not, 8- and 10-year-olds are less likely than adults to judge that *"Molly pressed the doorbell, because it rang"* is less acceptable than *"Molly pressed the doorbell, so it rang"* (Cain & Nash, 2011). Children aged 10 years and over are more likely to understand the causal relationship between two events when it is signalled explicitly by the connective *because* (Irwin & Pulver, 1984). Studies such as these suggest that under certain circumstances, the presence of connectives aids the reader's ability to construct a coherent representation of the meaning of the text. In this way, a good understanding of the function of connectives may not only be useful for text comprehension in general, but may be particularly important to enable learning from informational texts across the curriculum.

Difficulties with cohesive ties: who has problems and why?

Pronouns. Even though pre-readers can use gender and other cues to understand pronouns, a number of studies show that poor comprehenders between about 7 and 10 years of age often have difficulties with them (e.g. Ehrlich, Rémond, & Tardieu, 1999; Oakhill & Yuill, 1986; Yuill & Oakhill, 1988). For instance, children with a specific comprehension deficit are less able than same-age good comprehenders to identify the antecedent for a personal pronoun in a simple sentence, such as *"Peter lent ten pence to Liz because she was poor"*, or to supply an appropriate personal pronoun in a sentence cloze task with similar materials (Oakhill & Yuill, 1986). As mentioned earlier, poor comprehenders typically also have problems when a text is read to them (i.e. in listening comprehension tasks) so it is no surprise that they also have problems understanding pronouns when they have to listen to short texts (Megherbi & Ehrlich, 2005). Thus, their difficulties with pronoun resolution are strongly linked to language comprehension skills more generally, and difficulties with pronoun resolution will contribute to poor comprehenders' difficulties with text integration and comprehension of text. Children might often use superficial cues to guide their interpretation of pronouns. For instance, Megherbi and Ehrlich (2005) found that while 8-year-old good comprehenders showed a preference for subject antecedents, same-age poor comprehenders showed a preference for object antecedents. For example, in the sentence: *"John* (subject) *finally spotted Peter* (object) *when he climbed the tree"*, the pronoun *he* is ambiguous, but the poor comprehenders chose *Peter* in preference to *John*. Objects are usually closer to the pronoun than subjects, so the poor comprehenders' preference indicates that they are focused on local cohesion rather than global coherence.

Memory limitations might be another reason why younger children and poor comprehenders have difficulties with pronouns. Megherbi and Ehrlich also found that poor comprehenders had a preference for close antecedents (e.g. *Peter* in the following sentence), whether or not they were correct, e.g. *"John finally spotted Peter after he put his glasses on."* This proximity effect highlights another influence on the accessibility of a referent: the distance between the pronoun and its antecedent, which is important because of the critical role that memory plays in the pronoun resolution process and both sentence- and text-level comprehension (Cain, 2007; Cain, Oakhill, & Bryant, 2004). In the case of pronoun understanding in particular, measures of working memory have been shown to be related to adults' ability to resolve pronouns (Daneman & Carpenter, 1980) and task manipulations that increase the memory load involved in pronoun resolution, such as preventing re-reading of the critical portion of text, adversely affect children's performance (Oakhill & Yuill, 1986). Thus, it is likely that memory skills might influence young children's ability to derive a secure mental model of the preceding text, which would enable them to correctly relate pronouns to their antecedents.

Connectives. Reading comprehension level affects children's ability to take advantage of connectives. This is evident when we examine children's storytelling: children with poor reading comprehension include few causal connectives (*because, so*) to link story events when narrating a made-up story (Cain, 2003). Similarly, children with poor reading comprehension are less likely to choose the correct temporal and causal connectives to fill in the spaces when connectives have been deleted from a story (Cain et al., 2005). Further, their incorrect choices are less likely to make sense than the errors made by same-age children with age-appropriate reading comprehension. This finding indicates that poor comprehenders may be less familiar with the precise meaning of (some) connectives. Further evidence for this conclusion comes from a study that examined the causal connective *because*. *Because* can be used to signal a causal link between two events, as in: *"Mary spilt the milk because John bumped into her."* The word *because* can also introduce evidence for a conclusion as in *"We can tell that Mary spilt the milk because there is a puddle on the floor."* Poor comprehenders were shown to have particular difficulties with the second deductive usage of *because* (Oakhill, Yuill, & Donaldson, 1990).

Together these studies suggest that poor comprehenders may be less aware of the function of particular connectives and also less familiar with the meanings of some connectives. They may not fully appreciate how these words signal the relations between events and, therefore, fail to be guided by connectives when reading. As a result, their comprehension is likely to suffer.

How to teach knowledge and use of cohesive ties

There are a number of reasons to believe that it is helpful for children to be taught examples of cohesive ties and their use during reading. Clearly, young readers need to understand the function of connectives and gain experience in the nature of relations that they signal. For example, *before* and *after* both signal temporality, but their meanings are distinct. Thus, activities that build up knowledge of how these different devices work is important. One way to do so is to present sentence pairs and to discuss appropriate connectives that might link their meanings and why, in a classroom discussion. Take the sentence pair: *"The bird flew off the branch. The cat was climbing the tree."* General knowledge enables children to consider the most appropriate temporal connective, e.g. "when" vs. "before" or "after", or causal connectives, e.g. "because". In this way, knowledge of the precise meanings of connectives can be consolidated.

Providing more general support for precise use of connectives may be useful in the classroom. Picture support has been shown to improve performance on a range of language tasks in research studies, and it also benefits the production of connectives in storytelling tasks. For example, when storytelling is supported by pictures that provide a clear sequence of causally related events, poor comprehenders include a greater number of causal connectives to link events (Cain, 2003). Similarly, when looking at the deductive use of *because*, using pictures to represent the events helps improve performance (Oakhill et al., 1990). Thus, pictures that clearly represent a temporal or causal chain of events may be beneficial in the classroom to help teach the meanings of connectives.

It is also important to consider how to draw children's attention to connectives when reading. One possibility is to highlight these words, particularly for children who may fail to use them to guide comprehension. A study of 10- and 12-year-olds found that comprehension improved when the connectives in a text had been underlined prior to reading and that even good readers benefited from this support (Geva & Ryan, 1985). Thus, it seems important to ensure robust knowledge of connectives and also to encourage children to attend to these words when reading.

There are also arguments in favour of teaching children about the functions of anaphoric links in text, and instructing them in how to interpret anaphors. There is a dearth of research in this area, probably because there is an assumption that children readily understand anaphors, particularly common ones such as personal pronouns, and the profound problems that some children have with these words are simply not appreciated. A general strategy that can be taught to children, which has been shown to support pronoun comprehension and use (as well as inference making), is mental imagery. This involves teaching children to imagine a story "like a movie" or "like pictures in your head" (Pressley, 1976). When poor readers are taught this strategy, their ability to correctly identify the antecedents of pronouns improves (Francey & Cain, in press).

There are several published guides to teaching children to use cohesive ties in reading (pronouns, lexical references, and connectives) (see Chapman, 1983, for an early example). However, there are too few scientific studies of the outcomes of such teaching to form a research base. A reason for this lack of studies may be that it makes little sense to teach children to use cohesive ties in isolation, that is, without also teaching children the logical structures of texts that are signalled by, e.g., connectives. This explanation is in line with Gallini, Spires, Terry, and Gleaton (1993) who explored which strategies would improve comprehension in high school poor readers. They compared three strategies, and showed that the effects of teaching the logical (hierarchical) structures of texts were significantly larger than those of teaching cohesive ties in isolation or a control strategy. The text structure group made greater advances in both reading comprehension and memory for texts than did the other two groups. However, no study has investigated the effects of teaching cohesive ties to children who are *also* taught text structure. Text structure and teaching text structure are topics of the next chapter.

Summary

This chapter provides an overview of the functions of cohesive links and anaphors in texts, and explains how they are important in helping the reader construct a coherent mental model during reading comprehension. Ways in which children's understanding of such links can be assessed and improved are also considered.

Glossary

Anaphor: Anaphors include pronouns (*he, she, it, them*) and verb phrase ellipsis (*"She won't have another slice of cake, but he will [elided verb phrase: have another slice of cake]."*) and take their meaning from another part of the text (its antecedent).

Cohesive tie: A word or phrase that signals a link between parts of a text. Cohesive ties include connectives, but the term is broader and can refer to lexical links in a text – e.g. "the sea … the waves" and anaphors.

Connective: Connectives are cohesive devices that can explicitly signal the nature of the relation between events in a text. They can indicate temporal, causal, and contrastive events, as well as continuity.

Metacognition: Higher-level thinking (i.e. thinking about thinking) that enables the individual to understand, analyse, and actively control their processing, for example reflecting on the adequacy of one's memory or understanding of a text.

Phonological processing: The processing of auditory information: speech. This is involved in remembering spoken language and tasks that tap someone's awareness of the sound structure of words (phonological awareness, e.g. which words rhyme: fish, dish, goat).

Suggested answers to activities

Activity 6.1 Pronoun resolution
• What does each of the pronouns refer to in these examples?

- How did you know?
  - *Peter lent his car to Paul because <u>he</u> had missed the last train.* He is likely to refer to Paul, because Peter would have needed the car if he had missed the train.
  - *Peter lent his car to David because <u>he</u> had a broken ankle.* He is likely to refer to Peter because the broken ankle made him unable to drive his car.
  - *Nicki pulled the dagger from the corpse. <u>It</u> had a silver handle. <u>It</u> was a probably that of a burglar.* The first *it* refers to the dagger because daggers have handles. The second *it* refers to the corpse, because people, not daggers, can be burglars.
  - *Eve asked the surgeon if <u>she</u> knew which finger was causing trouble.* She is likely to refer to the surgeon because the question is about a diagnosis. Only a minority of surgeons are female so understanding the pronoun may not be automatic.

Activity 6.2 Lexical links
- The lexical links connect: exercise – bike rides – racing bike – riding, and spare time – evening – weekend – lunch hour.
- The two semantic networks can be named "spare time" and "cycling".

Activity 6.3 The power of connectives
1 *John was late <u>because</u> he was going to Helen's place.* John was *not* eager to get there, so perhaps he is not so fond of Helen.
2 *John was late <u>although</u> he was going to Helen's place.* John was *eager* to get to Helen's place, so perhaps he is fond of Helen.
3 *John was late <u>so</u> he was going to Helen's place.* Going to Helen's place must involve saving time, or perhaps she is a night owl, or someone whom he knows very well and can visit even at late hours.
4 *John was late <u>or</u> he was going to Helen's place.* This is a very different situation because the writer does not know what John is doing. John is not where the writer expects him to be. He is likely to go to Helen's place, perhaps even regularly, if this is to be any explanation of his unexpected absence.

Activity 6.4 Select the connective
- Insert the connectives that provides the most likely meaning in each of these examples:

  1 Paula searched for her gloves [why? *because, as*] it was cold in the morning.
  2 Paula searched for her gloves [when? *before, prior to*] leaving the house.
  3 Paula searched for her gloves [why in the world? *although, even though*] she knew it was warm outside.
  4 Paula searched for her gloves [what happened? *so, consequently*] she missed the bus.

7

FINDING AND USING TEXT STRUCTURE WHEN READING

> "Minnie blinks and reads the sentence again.... Can this really be the beginning of a story? She turns back a page to confirm that indeed it is.... Minnie is used to stories where you are told at the outset who is who – what the names of the heroine and hero are, and where they live, and what they look like – before the story proper gets going."
>
> *Author Author!, David Lodge (2004, p. 20)*

The character in this extract is having some difficulty understanding a short story. Of relevance to this chapter is her expectation that traditional stories follow a pattern: they have a beginning, a middle, and an end, and the introductory sentences typically announce the key characters, setting, and critical information, which serve as a foundation for the story. It is not just narrative texts that have recognisable structures; informational (or expository) texts follow a variety of formats that indicate how ideas will be presented in relation to each other, e.g. sequential vs. compare and contrast. In this chapter, we will consider how knowledge of the structure or format of different texts may be used to guide comprehension.

The purposes of this chapter are:

- to attract attention to the importance of how texts are built and how knowledge of text structure is a great help for building comprehension,
- to allow the readers to become familiar with a range of general text structures that can be found in both narrative and informational texts,
- to suggest ways in which such structures can be taught to even beginner readers.

Two broad text genres: narrative vs. informational (expository) texts

Text genres are conventional types of texts that are used for specific purposes of communication. For example, fairy tales, news articles, timetables, blogs, and emails are all different genres. Each genre has one or more conventional structures, which can influence comprehension (Zwaan, 1994). Readers who are familiar with the particular structure of the genre of the text have several advantages: they know what to expect from different parts of the text, where to search for particular types of information, and how the different parts of the text are linked together. For example, fairy tales are a classic kind of narrative. They begin "once upon a time", an idyll is disrupted, and it takes the hero three brave attempts to restore the idyll for which he is rewarded with the princess and half of the kingdom so that "they live happily ever after". News articles may follow several different structures each with their conventions.

A primary distinction in text genre is that between narrative (typically, stories) and informational (expository), where the purpose is to inform, describe, or explain content.

Narratives concern characters, their actions, their mental states and emotions, their interactions with others in the text and also with the physical world of the narrative, and have a narrative "point of view". There are several features common to a typical story: an *introduction* to orient the reader, which usually describes the main characters and setting, for example a young child living in the Russian countryside; an *initiating event*, such as losing a pet dog; the character's *goal* to find that pet and the *motivation* for that action, because this was a much-loved dog and the loss has made the child sad; often there is a *problem* or a conflict that must be *resolved* so that the main characters can accomplish their goal, for example the pet getting into a dangerous situation from which it must be rescued, such as seeking shelter in a cave and disturbing a fierce bear. More sophisticated stories also include consequences and reactions to the outcome and also unexpected situations or complications (Stein & Glenn, 1982).

Informational (expository) texts can follow a range of structures, such as description, sequence, compare and contrast, problem–solution, and cause–effect, and often a text will combine two or more of these structures (Meyer & Freedle, 1984). Thus, a text about the constitutional monarchy in the UK could simply describe the system currently in place, or how monarchies first arose across Europe, or the text might additionally explain the current UK system through examples of what is similar and also what is different between the UK's ceremonial constitutional monarchy and an executive system, such as the one in place in Monaco. Each of these structures of description, sequence, and compare and contrast might be found in the same text. An overview of these different structures and some of the signal words common to each is provided in Table 7.1. Because informational texts often contain unfamiliar concepts and vocabulary, they can require high levels of inference skill. Therefore, an appreciation of the structure and how

TABLE 7.1   An overview of different informational text structures and their signal words. Graphic diagrams for these structures are shown in Activity 7.4

Type	Description	Signal words
Description	A topic is described by listing various characteristics, features, and also examples.	To illustrate; the characteristics are; for instance; for example; also; such as …
Sequence	Items are presented in an order, typically chronological.	First, second, third; then; next; before, after; finally
Compare and contrast	Two or more items are presented and how they are similar and also different is discussed.	Different from; same as; on the other hand; in contrast to
Cause and effect	One or more causes and effects are detailed.	Because; since; as a result; accordingly; may be due to; reasons why
Problem and solution	A problem is stated and various solutions are then presented.	The problem is; a solution is; the question is; one answer is

it signals connections between ideas is crucial to successful understanding of these texts and also to learning from them.

An overview of informational text structures

There are other features of informational (expository) texts that may cause children comprehension difficulties if they are not familiar with this broad genre and its conventions. Informational texts typically use timeless verb constructions, e.g. *"Bears live in caves"* rather than *"The bear lived in a cave"*, which is typical of narrative. Informational texts often communicate about new situations and knowledge bases, thus there may be more technical vocabulary and unfamiliar concepts to understand. Thus, early exposure to informational texts is a good thing (Duke, 2000).

Activity 7.1 Identify the structure

- Identify the structure of each of these four texts:

  A   In developing countries, military expenses are closely linked to infant mortality. A relatively high spending on weapons means that less money is going into education, health, and infrastructure. As a result, access to quality healthcare, clean water, and basic foods becomes limited. This puts vulnerable humans, such as infants, at higher risk. In the long run, high military expenses also impede economic growth, which may lead into a negative spiral of unemployment, violence, and further threats to infants.

  B   Many houses were originally built at a proper distance from the road. As roads have been expanded, these houses are now very close to the roads, and the rooms facing the roads can be plagued with noise. New noise insulating windows and wall covers may reduce the noise substantially. Another solution is to use new road surfaces containing mixes of rubber so that the traffic does not create as much noise.

  C   There are many reasons to buy organic food rather than conventionally produced food. The most commonly stated reason is that organic foods are thought to be healthier. However, this is rarely found in proper studies of comparable products. The main difference is that organic foods are produced in ways that are less stressful for the animals and environments involved. Less intensive farming costs more, so organic food is usually more expensive.

  D   General Custard immediately realised that he had come up against powers he could not handle when he met Lydia. His heart made a double somersault, and his six-pack sagged. His stock of commands was useless. He made a valiant search for words in the midst of a galloping stutter.

- How did you identify the structures?
- Which of the signal words from Table 7.1 did you find?

How to assess an individual's knowledge of text structure

The assessment of narrative text structure can take many forms, including: questions about typical text features; ratings of the quality of narratives produced by children; and story sequencing tasks. These will be described briefly, in turn.

As stated above, there are features common to narratives and we can assess how well children understand these conventions by asking them questions such as "Is there anything special about the first one or two sentences in a story? What do they tell you?" (Paris & Jacobs, 1984). Such questions may be hard for children, particularly young children, to answer without a concrete example, so teachers can use probe questions to tap understanding of the key elements after a narrative reading, such as "What happened to get the story started?" More examples of these questions, prompts, and responses can be found in Table 7.2.

Another technique to assess knowledge of narrative structure is to ask children to narrate a story and then to score the responses for the inclusion of key elements and how well the events and ideas are related. Four-year-olds tend to produce character- or temporally-bound narratives, in which all the events happen to a single character or in a fixed location and are rather descriptive in nature. By 8 to 10 years of age children produce more sophisticated event sequences with plot development, such that events are causally related and include problems and resolutions that enable goals to be achieved (Stein & Glenn, 1982). Producing stories, whether written or oral, can be hard for young children, so prompts may be used to aid storytelling. These prompts can include picture sequences or the retelling of a story after it has been read out to the child. The narratives produced by the child can be assessed for cohesion between sentences (see Chapter 6) and coherence between story episodes, as well as memory for key events in the case of retells (Cain, 2003; Shapiro & Hudson, 1997). Examples of stories produced by children of different ages and ability levels and ways to analyse them are provided in Activity 7.2.

Activity 7.2 How well structured are these stories?

* Below are three short narratives told by young readers at different levels of comprehension ability. Your task is to consider how well structured they are. Look for examples of local cohesion, coherence in place and time, causal relatedness, and for narrative structure.

    A   The Fishing Trip. One day a little girl and her mum and dad went on a fishing trip. Her dad tried to catch fish. He didn't get any. He sat there all day and caught none at all. Then the little girl saw some birds. She chucked bread out for them. Her mum told her not to. The little girl was naughty and chucked the bread out for the birds anyway. Suddenly there were lots of fish. They liked the bread. And then her dad tried again and all the fish came to him. At last, her dad caught a fish. The End.

    B   Once upon a time this girl and a boy and her mum and dad went to the circus and they saw a clown. I would like to be a clown, and I would have a big red

> nose and long floppy shoes. And I would make people laugh. You can buy ice cream at a circus. There are also elephants, sometimes. Once my dad bought me the biggest ice cream I have ever had. It was strawberry flavour. The end.
>
> C One day a boy went to the shops and he saw a poster about a circus coming to town and on Monday he went down to the Big Top and he met a clown and the clown said "would you like to come to the circus" and the little boy said "yes" so he walked his dog into the Big Top and he bought some popcorn and some crisps and watched the circus. The clown that he met a few minutes ago was funny and the lions were scary and after it had finished he went home and had his tea.

Another way to assess understanding of narrative structure, and one that has lower memory demands than a story production task, is a macro-cloze task. A cloze task is an assessment in which texts have certain words removed and the task is to replace the missing word, for example, *"The farmer _____ some hay to the horse."* In a macro-cloze task, more than a single word is missing. To use a macro-cloze task to assess knowledge of story structure, children are read (or read for themselves) a story that has a key element missing, for example, a beginning and a character's reaction but no setting, and they are asked to supply the missing information. How well the child's response fits the category of missing information can be used to indicate the extent of their knowledge of typical narrative structure (Whaley, 1981).

TABLE 7.2 Examples of prompts and multiple-choice questions to assess children's understanding of narrative structure

What happens to get the story started?

What did _____ do about _____?

What makes it difficult for the character(s) to solve their problem?

Does anyone help the main character(s) solve the problem?

How is the problem solved?

What does the title of a story tell you?

Choose from:
a) What the words in the story are.
b) Who wrote the story.
c) What the story is about.
d) Whether the story is interesting.

What information is typically found at the end of a story?

Choose from:
a) How the main character's problem is solved.
b) How the characters' lives go on after the story.
c) The lessons that can be learned from the story.
d) Any (or all) of the above.

Finally, story structure knowledge can be assessed without the need for the child to plan and narrate the story at all. To do this, researchers have presented children with the events or episodes of a story in a jumbled order and asked them to re-arrange them so that the sequence "tells a good story". For younger children, this can take the form a sequence of pictures; for older children who can read, the information can be presented as separate story sentences to be rearranged (Cain, 1996; Oakhill & Cain, 2012; Stein & Glenn, 1982).

Assessments of *informational text* structure often focus on broader language and comprehension skills such as recall and how well the content is understood, rather than an awareness of critical textual features (Hall, Markham, & Culatta, 2005). One method used to assess appreciation of text structure is to present two-sentence stimulus passages that map onto a particular structure, such as description or compare and contrast. Participants are then asked to judge whether additional sentences are a good fit to the paragraph. The target good-fit sentences expand on this information; the poor-fit distractor sentences introduce new information (Englert & Hiebert, 1984). The idea behind this method is that children who are sensitive to a particular structure will activate appropriate schemas when reading the initial information and use that information to organise subsequent information. Thus, in this assessment, they will be "primed" for structure-relevant material and be more likely to judge that as an appropriate continuation, when it occurs. Examples of such an assessment are provided in Table 7.3.

Given that informational text structures have key signal words that are essential for comprehending the relations between ideas presented in the text (see Table 7.1), it seems important to establish that these terms are understood as well, and teachers may wish to include such an assessment if they are concerned about poor appreciation of informational text. Indeed, in their work on the relation between knowledge of text structure and comprehension, Williams and colleagues included tests to measure knowledge of the critical clue words taught in informational text structure lessons, to check that children had learned these words during the instruction component (Williams, Stafford, Lauer, Hall, & Pollini, 2009).

TABLE 7.3 Examples of materials used to assess sensitivity to different informational text structures. Only the target sentences follow the original text structure (text onset)

Sentence type	Compare and contrast
Text onset ("prime")	Dogs can get colds just like people do. When a dog gets a cold it sneezes.
Continuation	Dogs' noses run just like people's do.
Continuation	Dogs get watery eyes, just like the eyes of a person with a cold.
Distractor	Dogs come in all different shapes and sizes.
Distractor	The dachshund has very short legs and a long body.
Judgements	• Yes, that sentence belonged with that passage. • Yes, that sentence sort of belonged with the passage. • Not sure, that sentence did not really belong with that passage. • No, that sentence did not belong with that passage.

Source: Adapted from Englert and Hiebert (1984).

Activity 7.3 Build upon the structure

- The text below has a cause–effect structure. Follow this structure when you continue the text. Your contribution can be a further consequence and/or an addition to the causes. Also, try to make sentences that do not fit with the structure but are still on the same topic. You can create examples for both teaching and assessment similar to those in Table 7.3 above.

Sentence type	Cause and effect
Text onset	Traffic accidents are the most common cause of traumatic head injury. Cyclists are particularly vulnerable. Brain damage following head injury frequently causes sensory and motor problems and serious language impairments from which full recovery is rare.
Continuation (consequence)	(Example: Staff at NHS brain injury departments all wear helmets when they ride a bicycle.)
Continuation (consequence)	
Continuation (cause)	
No causal connection	

The development of knowledge and use of text structure

Most children are familiar with fictional narratives before they start school through picture books, shared book reading, cartoons and movies, and even nursery rhymes. They are also familiar with narrative structure through relating autobiographical accounts of events such as birthday parties, trips to the doctor, and holidays. There is a strong relation between understanding of narratives in different forms: children's ability to understand the causal relations between events in a televised narrative, such as a cartoon, is related to their ability to identify causal relations in stories read aloud (Kendeou, van den Broek, White, & Lynch, 2009). The same is true for adults: comprehension of written texts, spoken texts, and static cartoon sequences are highly related (Gernsbacher, Varner, & Faust, 1990).

Although most young children are familiar with the typical structure and common themes of narratives, narratives provide a vehicle for children to explore different places, cultures, problems, and solutions that they may not encounter in their everyday lives. However, we typically consider storybooks as a form of entertainment. Understanding a character's goals is essential for following the chain of actions in a narrative and connecting events. A goal motivates the following actions. So, in response to losing his pet frog in the story *Frog, Where Are You?*, the main character's superordinate goal is to find his frog, which motivates the actions in the first episode (Mayer, 1969). Adult comprehenders rate goals in a narrative as more important than other elements and they are also more likely to include these in their recalls (Mandler & Johnson, 1977; van den Broek, Lorch, & Thurlow, 1996). However, pre-schoolers are more likely to recall concrete events such as actions, rather than internal states, such as goals (van den Broek et al., 1996). Sensitivity to goals is apparent in young children if the text strongly supports them: children as young as 6 years of age make goal-directed inferences when the text is considerate and supports this type of inference (Lynch & van den Broek, 2007).

As stated above, children's comprehension of stories presented in different media is related: children who are good at answering questions about the theme and key causal events in a televised cartoon are also good at answering similar questions about a story that has been read out to them (Lynch et al., 2008). Narrative skills assessed with such methods are predictive of later reading comprehension ability. Researchers have found that 6-year-olds' ability to recall the key events in stories read aloud and also televised cartoons predicts their reading comprehension 2 years later (Kendeou et al., 2009). For slightly older children, the ability to correctly order a sequence of sentences to "tell a good story" when aged 7 to 8 years predicts their reading comprehension 3 years later (Oakhill & Cain, 2012). This work demonstrates the importance of narrative knowledge as a foundation for broader text comprehension skills.

Informational texts are not used to the same extent as narratives in the early years classroom, although educational researchers have long argued for their inclusion for both interest and practical reasons (Duke, 2000). However, pre-readers are familiar with this genre. They show a sensitivity to the different language and structural features of narrative and informational genres; when pretend re-reading books from each genre, clear differences between the two are apparent, reflecting different types of book language (Pappas, 1993). Informational texts are used more widely in the curriculum in the later school years as a primary source of learning, and constitute about 75% of school reading material by secondary school (Venezky, 2000). Informational texts typically contain new facts and information and will, therefore, often concern concepts and knowledge areas that are not familiar to the young reader. Thus, it is no surprise that background knowledge of a topic is one of the principle predictors of comprehension of informational text (Best, Floyd, & McNamara, 2008). Williams and colleagues (Williams et al., 2009) have shown that informational text use in the primary classroom is an excellent vehicle for building background knowledge.

Appreciation of informational text structure has been assessed with judgement of possible continuations to short passages with different structures, as described above (Englert & Hiebert, 1984). When assessed in this way, age differences in sensitivity to structure are apparent: children aged between 8 and 9 years are not as able to differentiate between the sentences that fit and do not fit as children 3 years older. If children are sensitive to a particular structure, they will activate that rapidly on reading the first sentence or two of a text, recognising the signal words and style, and be able to use their knowledge to structure the subsequent information in memory, aiding comprehension and recall. Thus, good knowledge and appreciation of informational text structure should help to guide comprehension of this genre.

Difficulties with text structure: who has problems and why?

As noted above, narrative skills are related to concurrent and later reading comprehension ability. Thus, it is not surprising to find that children with poor reading comprehension often do poorly on assessments of narrative. Why is this the case?

Despite the extensive exposure children have to narratives from an early age, children with poor reading comprehension appear to be less knowledgeable about how narratives work. For example, their responses to questions about settings and endings and the purpose of story titles are less detailed and more vague than those of good comprehenders (Cain, 1996). It may be the case the children with poor comprehension are simply less able to provide detailed explanations, but they show impoverished knowledge of stories in other tasks as well. For example, when shown a simple story that is depicted with four or five pictures and asked to select a statement that best described what the story was about, poor comprehenders are less likely to differentiate between statements about settings, characters, and the main point of the story (Yuill & Oakhill, 1991). Poor comprehenders also have difficulties producing a causally related narrative unless given help in the form of picture prompts or a very explicit goal to drive the narrative action (Cain, 2003).

Clearly, a difficulty with explaining key parts of stories and producing oral and written narratives may be due, in part, to problems with planning and memory. The finding that picture sequences and goal-directed prompts improve performance supports that explanation. However, the failure to appreciate the main point of a story suggests that children with comprehension difficulties also fail to make connections between the critical events in a story and represent these in a structured, hierarchical fashion, in order to extract the essence or gist. In the work described earlier on narrative development, the critical feature of televised and aurally presented stories that predicted later reading comprehension was an understanding of the causal relations between events (Kendeou et al., 2009).

There has been far less research on poor comprehenders' difficulties with informational text. When comparing high and low achievers of secondary school age, low achievers show poorer awareness of a range of text structures (using the continuation judgement task described earlier). Further, they are also less likely to produce structure-appropriate continuations from an initial prompt than higher-achieving peers (Englert & Thomas, 1987). Children with greater awareness of informational text structure appear to use this to remember information when reading: their recall of well-formed text is superior to scrambled text, whereas children with poor awareness are not aided by a well-formed text (Taylor & Samuels, 1983). Good knowledge of informational text structure appears to support the representation of information in an organised and related manner.

How to foster knowledge and use of text structure

Teaching children about text structure can help them to sequence information when reading and listening and it can be taught in the early years classroom. As noted earlier, young children are familiar with narrative from a young age and can sequence pictures and understand the sequence of and relations between events in picture books and televised cartoons. One instructional method used with students aged between 6 and 7 years is to teach explicit "tricks" to help them to understand fiction (Paris & Paris, 2007). The methods taught in this study included a "five-finger trick" to help them to remember the five key elements of narrative: settings, character, initiating event, problem, resolution-ending; strategies to support inference making about critical aspects of narrative such as feelings, thoughts, and themes; and a "recipe" for retelling narratives with a beginning, middle, and end.

Children taught these techniques subsequently included a greater number of key narrative elements in story retellings and had better story comprehension than those who were not given this explicit instruction. Further, the benefits were found for the comprehension of narratives presented as picture books and also for stories read aloud to the children. Of interest, the effects were specific to narrative; comprehension of informational text did not improve differentially for the narrative instruction and control groups. This study by Paris and Paris suggests that instruction that is specific to different genres is important.

There is increasing interest in instruction in informational text structures because of its importance for learning from text. Such instruction does not need to be contained within a literacy lesson, but can form part of a history, science, or geography lesson, so that the text structure instruction is embedded in learning. Successful instruction that has used this framework has been shown to be effective with children as young as 8 years of age (Williams et al., 2007, 2009). Lesson content includes: the teaching of key words that are critical for a particular text structure, which signal how information is related, such as *alike, both, compare, but, however, contrast*; the use of specific questions, such as *What two things is this paragraph about? How are they alike? How are they different?*; the use of graphic organisers to structure information; and writing summaries of the content.

Graphic organisers are powerful tools for the teaching of text structure and reading comprehension (National Reading Panel, 2000). They have the advantage over plain text in that they directly visualise abstract relations (including inferences as shown in Chapter 4). Some frequently used graphic organisers are shown in Activity 7.4 below.

Activity 7.4 Make the text structure visible

- Compare the graphic organisers below to the text structures listed in Table 7.1. Which of the graphic organisers can be used to visualise each text structure in Table 7.1 (page 83)?

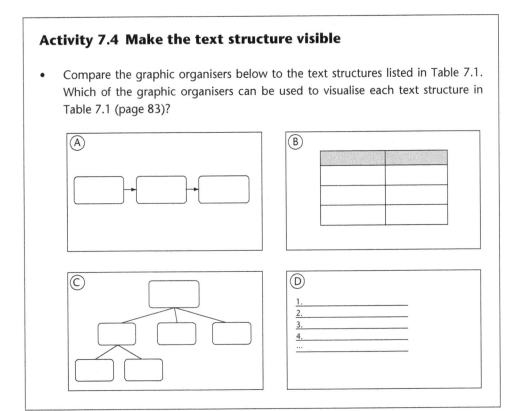

Summary

Knowledge of different text structures is useful for guiding comprehension, particularly of new material. It helps the reader to establish critical relations between information, whether causal relations in narrative or informational text. Children with poor reading comprehension appear to lack both knowledge of different structural features and also how to apply such knowledge, but recent instructional studies demonstrate that this knowledge can be taught successfully to beginner readers. Thus, we would recommend that teachers consider text structure in a range of lessons, not just in reading and literacy lessons. It would be beneficial to use graphic organisers to help children to visualise these different structures. Further, they can be taught how different words signal how to make links between different parts of the text. Through this, knowledge and use of text structure can support constructive processing of the situation model.

Glossary

Narrative texts are usually fiction, i.e. made up. They concern characters, their actions, their mental states and emotions, their interactions with others in the text and also with the physical world of the narrative.

Informational texts, also called *expository* texts, include textbooks, most web pages, discussion forums, journal articles. Such texts are *meant* to inform, discuss, describe, or explain content. However, in some cases they may be *read* as narratives. One example are news *stories*, which report real events, but may use the dramatic present tense ("Man bites dog!") and other narrative techniques to provide the reader with a more exciting experience.

Suggested answers to activities

Activity 7.1. Identify the structure

A   This text is about a *cause* (military expenses) and its *effects*. Some of the words and phrases that signal cause and effects are *closely linked to, means, as a result, may lead into.*

B   This text has a *problem–solution* structure. The problem is the noise in houses that are very close to roads. A signal word is <u>solution</u>, but there are also opposites like *plagued with noise, reduce noise,* and *not . . . as much noise*. The opening of the text has a cause–effect structure.

C   The structure is *compare and contrast* (organic vs. conventionally produced foods). Signal words are *main difference, however, less, more.*

D   This text is basically a *description* (of Custard's responses to Lydia). Although the text has none of the signal words of descriptive texts, it *illustrates* and *exemplifies* Custard's early symptoms of a severe emotional crush. The particular sequence of these symptoms is less important to the meaning of the text.

The underlined words are listed as signal words in Table 7.1.

Activity 7.2 How well structured are these stories?

A   This is a fully formed story. It has a setting, a causally connected series of events, and a conclusion that reflects back on the introduction.

B   This is not a fully formed story. It does have a theme, but little cohesion in place and time. The sentences are not causally related, but appear to be random associations on the theme. The text has no narrative structure and no conclusion.

C   This is an "and-then-and-then" story, an intermediate story. It is coherent in time and place. However, the long list of events is merely related in chronological order. The story lacks causal relatedness and narrative structure.

Activity 7.3 Build upon the structure

- A continuation of the text following its cause-and-effect structure might be: Campaigns to make cyclists wear helmets could save many people each year from death or life-long handicaps and would also save significant hospital resources.

- No causal connection: A discontinuation of the structure might venture into a description of bicycles or brain injuries, for example: Bicycles are excellent for both the cyclist's fitness and the environment.

Activity 7.4 Make the text structure visible

A   Cause and effect

B   Compare and contrast

C   Description

D   Sequence

8

DOES IT MAKE SENSE?
MONITORING FOR MEANING

"Mog wasn't really reading properly, and recognising this, kept turning back to the beginning of the chapter, trying and failing to make the sentences adhere."

The White Lie, Andrea Gillies (2012, p. 99)

The character, Mog, in this extract is distracted and not able to focus fully on what she is reading. As a result, Mog is experiencing problems in understanding what she is reading. Pertinent to our focus here, it is clear from this description that Mog is a skilled (adult) comprehender: she recognises that she is not combining ideas and failing making sense of the text. In short, she is monitoring her comprehension and appreciates that she has not fully understood what she is reading. She is also a strategic reader who is taking remedial action by turning back the pages and re-reading.

The purposes of this chapter are:

- to stress the importance of comprehension monitoring – online checking that the text makes sense – and ways to repair comprehension problems,
- to provide insight into what makes it difficult for children to monitor their comprehension,
- to suggest ways in which comprehension monitoring can be improved through teaching.

What is comprehension monitoring?

Comprehension monitoring occurs when the reader (or listener) reflects on his or her own understanding. So, as in the example above, one aspect of comprehension monitoring is being aware as to whether the text makes sense. Examples of the types of question that a reader might ask him- or herself when reflecting on understanding are provided in Table 8.1.

You can probably recall experiences of your own comprehension monitoring: have you ever turned over a page and found that what you are reading does not make sense?

TABLE 8.1 Comprehension monitoring: examples of questions to help comprehension monitoring

- Does that make sense?
- Why did she do that?
- Why did he say that?
- How does this connect with the first part of the story?
- How does this information fit with what I already know about this topic?

Most likely, you turned over two pages by mistake, so you could not integrate the text you were currently reading with what you read on the preceding page. Another common instance of monitoring is when you come across an unfamiliar word, as in *"She liked the mirror frame because it was arcate"*, and *"I could never keep a dog, because of their olid presence."* People who are good at comprehension monitoring are aware of the adequacy of their understanding as they read or listen to a text. They may also use a range of strategies, such as re-reading or looking up the meaning of difficult word, when they experience comprehension difficulty (Pressley & Afflerbach, 1995). Thus, to be effective comprehenders, readers must be able to assess their understanding of what they read and also know what strategies to apply if they detect a failure to understand. Examples of strategies that may be useful when comprehension fails are provided in Table 8.2.

A failure to understand a text adequately can arise for many different reasons. For example, comprehenders may lack relevant knowledge: they may not know the meanings of critical words that are central to the main ideas; they may have poor knowledge of linguistic devices that indicate the causal sequence of events; or they may lack relevant background knowledge to provide a framework for the ideas presented in the text. If comprehenders are able to monitor for sense, there is an opportunity to fix any errors in understanding, provided they have the strategic knowledge. In this way, being aware of how well one understands a text is a first step towards ensuring adequate comprehension. However, young children and those with language and literacy difficulties may find it hard to monitor their understanding, because comprehension monitoring depends on cognitive resources such as memory and attention. This idea will be further developed in the section on the comprehension monitoring skills of children who have reading comprehension difficulties.

Assessment of comprehension monitoring

There are many different ways to assess an individual's ability to monitor their comprehension. One method, favoured by researchers, is to deliberately insert errors in a text. Examples of different errors are given in Activity 8.1 below.

Errors that have been used in research (and illustrated in Activity 8.1) include made-up (nonsense) words, scrambling the words in a sentence, including a fact that conflicts with prior knowledge, and inserting two contradictory pieces of information (proposi-

---

TABLE 8.2 Fix-up strategies that can be used when things do not make sense

---

When you fail to understand a word, you might: check that you have pronounced it correctly; try to work out its meaning by analysing its morphological constituents (e.g. *un-miss-able*) or using inference from contextual cues; look up its meaning in a dictionary; read on to see if its meaning is clarified.

When you fail to understand the reason for a character's actions, you might: re-read that part of the story; read on to see if a reason is provided; generate a plausible inference.

Note. Someone may be good at monitoring their comprehension but not be good at applying fix-up strategies.

---

tions). If readers detect an error, it indicates that they are engaged in comprehension monitoring.

Activity 8.1 Spot the errors. Examples of assessments of comprehension monitoring

- Read these five short texts. Which of them do not make sense and why?

  A   Cinderella shook her head slowly when she looked at her new doll. She did not get on with the others and her fod was too short.
  B   Four card players were seated near the bar. One of the players was about to make a bid of two spades were left in the shed.
  C   This dish with fried eggs is quite simple and takes only 10 minutes. You simply peel them and slice them up for your sandwich.
  D   The move from skiing to snowboarding was something Dan had been looking forward to for half the season. Conditions had been poor, but with the rain forecast he would hit the slopes in a few days.
  E   When the architect saw the upturned coffee table, she knew that the owner was ready to sell. She made an offer that was far below the market price.

To assess whether or not an error has been detected, researchers typically ask the child whether or not a text makes sense. By including consistent or error-free texts in an assessment, in addition to texts with errors, the assessor can be sure that the child differentiates between those texts that do make sense – are coherent – and those that do not. It is also useful to find out whether the child can identify the part (or parts) that does not make sense. A reader can only try to fix a miscomprehension if s/he is aware of *why* comprehension failed. This technique – of asking whether or not a text makes sense and, if not, why not – can also be used by teachers in the classroom, to find out if a child has experienced difficulty with any words or concepts.

Clearly, by asking a child if a story makes sense or not, the teacher (or researcher, indeed) may alert the child to the existence of errors or incongruencies and may encourage the type of strategic processing that they would not typically engage in everyday reading. For the purposes of assessment, however, this activity indicates the child's *potential* to detect errors and monitor their comprehension.

Activity 8.1 gave some examples of different errors in texts. Clearly, most authors are considerate and do not insert errors into texts. What is important to think about are the different types of evaluation required by readers in order to monitor for sense. For example, to identify that a word is not known, readers must check that they know the meaning of each word; to determine that a statement does not fit with prior knowledge, readers must compare the sense of what has been read with what they already know about a particular scenario or topic; and to detect a conflict between two propositions, readers must check the sense of what they have just read with the mental model of the text's meaning that they have constructed so far, thus they must be engaging in an attempt to integrate each new proposition into their mental model. This level of "checking" is not necessarily deliberate for skilled comprehenders; rather, the process of reading for meaning will mean that evaluation of comprehension on a range of levels takes place.

If a text does not make sense, for one of the reasons outlined above, the skilled comprehender can engage in remedial action to ensure good understanding. This may involve looking up an unknown word in a dictionary, re-reading a section of a text that does not make sense, and even generating an inference to enable integration between two propositions (see Table 8.2). Thus, the successful comprehender will not only detect when a failure to understand has occurred, but will also have the strategic knowledge to ensure that the text makes sense.

Away from the research lab, classroom materials and everyday reading books obviously do not have deliberately inserted errors, so what can you as a teacher do to determine if a child does not adequately monitor for sense? One possibility is to deliberately insert mistakes in texts that you read out loud to the child or group or to insert mistakes into specially prepared classroom materials. This might involve replacing a familiar word with an unknown word, deliberately misreading a sentence, and/or changing a proposition. Another possibility is simply to encourage children to summarise and retell parts of the text read or heard so far. You will then see if any miscomprehensions have occurred: did the child understand the main point, a character's motivations for a particular action, the causal sequence between events, etc.? Ways to encourage children to actively engage in comprehension monitoring will be discussed in the section "Teaching comprehension monitoring". A third option is to ask children to rate each section of a text for difficulty. Provided that the text is of variable difficulty, children should not rate it all as easy. The rating can be combined with different tasks, such as detection of unfamiliar words, ideas that are hard to integrate into a mental model, etc.

The development of comprehension monitoring: what can children do and when?

Children are able to monitor for sense from an early age, before they begin formal reading instruction. For example, children aged between 3 and 4 years show surprise, a sign of monitoring, when an actor or the temporal order of events is changed during the

TABLE 8.3 Explicit and implicit inconsistencies (Markman, 1979)

Explicit condition
Many different kinds of fish live in the ocean. Some fish have heads that make them look like alligators and some fish have heads that make them look like cats. Fish live in different parts of the ocean. Some fish live near the surface of the water, but some fish live way down at the bottom of the ocean. Fish must have light in order to see. There is absolutely no light at the bottom of the ocean. It is pitch black down there. When it is that dark the fish cannot see anything. They cannot even see colours. Some fish that live at the bottom of the ocean can see the colour of their food.
Note. The inconsistent information is underlined.

Implicit condition
as above until . . . There is absolutely no light at the bottom of the ocean. Some fish that live at the bottom of the ocean know their food by its colour. They will only eat red seaweed.

narration of a familiar storybook (Skarakis-Doyle, 2002). However, that does not mean that all children adequately monitor their comprehension all of the time. Take a look at the examples in Table 8.3, which were used in an early research study on comprehension monitoring in young readers. These are texts that contain internal inconsistencies. The inconsistency in this text may appear to be fairly obvious to you and me – if there is no light, the fish will not be able to see the colour of their food. However, 50% of 8- to 11-year-olds who took part in this study did not appear to notice the problem even in the explicit condition when asked questions such as "Did I forget to tell you anything?", and "Did everything make sense?". Performance in the implicit condition was far worse, with 96% of children failing to spot the problem.

The results of this study do not mean that comprehension monitoring is a late-developing skill. As we noted earlier, pre-readers are capable of monitoring for sense. The important message from this study is that comprehension monitoring does not always take place. There are several reasons why children may fail to spot what appear to be quite obvious problems with a text, such as those described above. One is that they may be reluctant to criticise texts provided by an adult. Indeed, when informed that some texts contain errors, which gives children permission to criticise, detection rates are found to improve. Another reason that children may appear not to monitor for meaning is that they may be using a different standard to the one targeted by the experimenter. In the study described, children's comments indicated that they were often engaging in moni-toring behaviour, but simply attending to other aspects of the text than those intended by the experimenter. For example, many children reported that they were checking that they knew the meanings of the words.

A study by Baker (1984) specifically investigated whether children were flexible in the standards they used to evaluate their comprehension. Children aged 5 to 11 years read texts with three different types of error: non-words (as a proxy of unfamiliar vocabulary items), information that was inconsistent with general knowledge, and internal inconsist-encies, which were similar to those studied by Markman (1979). Although children were told in advance that some of the texts contained errors, those aged up to 7 years found the internal inconsistencies particularly hard to spot. However, feedback and repeat pres-entations resulted in improved performance and most children were able to spot most of the errors.

These studies tell us that children can monitor their comprehension and adopt differ-ent standards of evaluation against their current vocabulary knowledge, general know-ledge, and the new information presented in the text. They also tell us that it is important to develop sensitive methods of assessment so that they do not underestimate young chil-dren's monitoring skills. Reasons for why young children may fail to adequately monitor their comprehension are discussed in the next section.

Comprehension monitoring difficulties: who has problems and why?

Young children and children with reading difficulties, particularly those with specific reading comprehension problems, often fail to monitor their comprehension adequately. Take a look at Activity 8.2.

Activity 8.2 Spot the inconsistencies

* Spot the errors in these two texts. Are they equally hard to spot?

Text one

The group of monkeys was searching the jungle looking for tasty things to eat. Their favourite nuts grew on the high branches of the tallest trees and there were none on the ground. The monkeys picked through the leaves and soil on the ground and collected up the tasty nuts. The baby monkeys ran and jumped around playing games together amongst the trees. The adult monkeys were always on guard, looking out for tigers that might attack them. When they had eaten all the nuts they moved on to find more food elsewhere.

Text two

The tiger walked slowly out of her den and looked back towards the two cubs sitting behind her. They had been born in early spring, so they were just a few weeks old. It was still early in the morning and it was quiet because there were no other animals about. She encouraged them to follow her, out of the den. At first they were timid, but they soon grew more confident. Their mother lay down on a sunny patch of grass a few metres away from the den and kept a close eye on them. She watched carefully as the cubs explored outside for the first time. They enjoyed playing in the warm autumn sun.

(Materials similar to those used by Oakhill, Hartt, & Samols, 2005).

Did you spot the errors? Why is the error in the second text harder to spot? This illustrates the types of texts used in a study by Oakhill and colleagues to compare the comprehension monitoring skills of two groups of children: one group comprised good readers, their word reading and reading comprehension were age-appropriate (as measured on a standardised assessment); the other group had problems with reading comprehension, their word reading was age-appropriate, but their ability to answer questions about those stories was weak.

The method used to study comprehension monitoring in this study was an inconsistency detection paradigm: in each text, two pieces of information were conflicting. In Activity 8.2, in the second text these two pieces were separated by several additional sentences. This increases the processing load needed to detect the inconsistency, because the comprehender does not simply compare information presented in two adjacent sentences but has to maintain a sufficiently accurate memory representation of the text in order to detect the conflict. When the memory load of a task is high, as in this instance, children with reading comprehension difficulties are less likely to identify which stories contain the errors (see Figure 8.1, which shows the number of correct identification of errors that children make in different memory load conditions). Given that young children have poorer memory skills than older children, memory limitations may, in part, explain why younger children typically detect fewer errors than do older children. We discussed the importance of memory for text processing skills in more detail in Chapter 2.

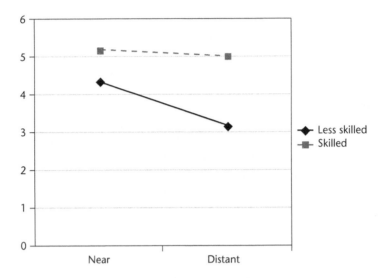

FIGURE 8.1 Less-skilled comprehenders have particular difficulties detecting incompatible pieces of information when they are separated by several sentences (data from Oakhill et al., 2005).

There are reasons other than the memory or attentional demands of the task that may influence how easily a child will spot a failure to comprehend. We mentioned the idea of setting different standards for monitoring earlier. A young child who is learning to decode or a poor word reader may focus on the word level to a greater extent than an older and more fluent reader. This is one reason why the younger readers are good at identifying nonsense or unfamiliar words in a text. Oakhill and colleagues have examined this standard of monitoring in poor comprehenders with good word reading skills, like the children described above. Similar to young readers, poor comprehenders do not evidence difficulties in detecting nonsense words in a text.

Young children do sometimes have difficulties identifying when the information in the text conflicts with their general knowledge about a topic. Stories like the one in Table 8.4 were presented to 5-, 6-, and 7-year-olds to by Tunmer and colleagues (Tunmer, Nesdale, & Pratt, 1983). Although this study demonstrated early monitoring abilities, the 5-year-olds found the implicit stories considerably more difficult than the explicit stories, with only 50% of the sample identifying a problem on six or more stories (out of eight). Background check questions such as "Can you ride a bicycle with broken wheels?" indicated that lack of relevant knowledge was not the reason for poor perform- ance. Tunmer and colleagues suggest that memory may be important: children had to

TABLE 8.4 Example of comprehension monitoring text used by Tunmer et al. (1983)

Explicit: You can't ride a bike with broken wheels. One morning a car ran over Johnny's bike and broke the wheel. Johnny then picked up his bike and rode it over to a friend's house.

Implicit: Johnny got a new bike for his birthday. One morning a car ran over Johnny's bike and broke the wheel. Johnny then picked up his bike and rode it over to a friend's house.

retrieve this information from their long-term memory and compare it with the information in the text to identify the problem. This type of monitoring activity and the need for
good memory skills may be particularly relevant when reading information texts, from
which the reader typically needs to learn new information to update what they already
know about a topic.

Together, the research on comprehension monitoring shows that children are able to
evaluate their comprehension from an early age, but their familiarity with the text or
topic area, the standard or task goal that they set, and also the memory and attentional
resources necessary to process text for meaning may all influence how well they do so.

Teaching comprehension monitoring

What can you as a teacher do to encourage children to monitor their understanding of
text? In research studies, we have seen how alerting children to the presence of errors is
one way to improve monitoring performance particularly if children are provided with
examples of the particular type of problem that might be present in a passage (Markman,
1979). This technique may be useful for modelling comprehension monitoring behaviours to show children examples of the types of problem they might encounter in naturalistic texts, such as unknown words, conflicts with prior knowledge, inconsistencies in
the text (to encourage evaluation of information within a text). By talking through our
own thought processes it becomes possible to identify the problem and consider what to
do (see Table 8.5 for an example of how this might work).

Good readers are active readers who engage with the text as they read and evaluate
their understanding both during and after reading. Thus, maybe it is simply necessary to
find ways to get poor comprehension monitors to engage with meaning construction
when reading. A study by de Sousa and Oakhill (1996) did just that. They found that
children with poor comprehension were much better at spotting nonsense words, conflicts with general knowledge, and internal inconsistencies when they were given the role
of a detective and instructed to read statements from people who were witnesses to a
crime compared to when they were simply reading passages and being asked to try to spot
the errors. Children with good reading comprehension were not influenced by the

TABLE 8.5 Example of a conversation to model comprehension monitoring behaviours (text
adapted from Yuill et al., 1989)

Jack's sister Julie was looking forward to a beach holiday with her friends. She was on a strict diet to
have the perfect bikini body. Jack was an excellent cook and liked having the family over for Sunday
lunch. This week he cooked his speciality dessert, Sticky Toffee Pudding. He was very proud of the
result. He knew that Julie loved Sticky Toffee Pudding. But he only had an apple for her.

Teacher: Does that make sense to you?

Child: Sure, why?

Teacher: I think that's a bit odd: Jack only had an apple for Julie.

Child: Because she liked apples!

Teacher: But it says here that she loved Sticky Toffee Pudding, and Jack knew.

Teacher: Can you find a clue in the story? Why does Jack serve Julie something else?

instructions: they were equally good at spotting errors whether they were playing at being a detective or simply told the standard instructions. The majority of texts do not fit easily into the detective/witness statement format, but this type of task may certainly be used to find out if a child with poor monitoring skills has the potential to develop good monitoring skills through engagement when reading and listening.

Activity 8.3 Dialogues to support comprehension monitoring

Below is a text and three children's responses to a question about its content. How could you help each of the children develop their comprehension monitoring? Suggest questions that might scaffold their development of comprehension monitoring.

The text: On a very sunny day, Big Al and his class were studying the life in a pond near the school. Alex's group had found a little creature with long legs that looked like oars, and came up to Al for help with the identification. Big Al, who was short sighted, had to put his glasses down, but then quickly identified the insect as a "water boatman". Al helped the group take a photo of the water boatman and put it back into the pond. There was a cracking noise in the grass behind them as Wayne came running with a bleeding nose. Oh, said Big Al, can someone help me find my glasses?

The question: What made the noise in the grass?
Child A: I don't know. Perhaps there was a dog?
Child B: What was the thing called – the water boatman?
Child C: Wayne stepped on something like a branch.

The de Sousa and Oakhill (1996) study provides some ideas about how monitoring might be enhanced in children who do not spontaneously or regularly check their comprehension. One method is to encourage children to summarise a text at set points while reading or listening. This is actually a good technique when studying (or reading a book like this): you cannot produce an adequate summary if you have not understood all of the main ideas and the act of summarising may help you to identify which bits are problematic.

Self-directed summarisation is one of the techniques taught by Palincsar and Brown (1984) in a package of skills designed to help children to both foster and monitor their comprehension. The package also included questioning, clarifying, and predicting and was taught using an interactive method in which the tutor modelled the behaviours to children in small groups, who gradually took over. With a tutor present, feedback can always be provided on the quality of an activity, for example, "Remember that a summary does not include all of the details. I would have summarised that part by saying…". Poor readers taught in this way subsequently produced better summaries than a control group and were also better on a transfer test of comprehension monitoring. Thus, teaching children to reflect on their understanding led to wider benefits.

A very different technique – encouraging children to visualise a story as a series of mental images – has also been shown to benefit comprehension monitoring. The idea is to teach children how to think about the text as a series of integrated pictures when reading or listening to a story. This technique is quick and easy to teach (Pressley, 1976) and aids memory for stories in typical readers and also poor comprehenders. In one study of poor readers, those who were taught to use mental imagery improved their ability to detect inconsistencies in a comprehension monitoring task (Gambrell & Bales, 1986). The improvement may have been because the use of mental images helped children to remember the details more accurately. Although very different from the summarisation method, a common core to both techniques is that success requires the comparison and integration of information from different parts of the text. Thus, instruction in mental imagery may improve comprehension monitoring success because it may encourage children to integrate information from each successive sentence, in order to incorporate the information into the image they were constructing.

Summary

This overview has shown that the ability to evaluate your understanding when reading or listening to text is an important skill. It is only if a failure to understand adequately is detected that the reader can try to repair it. Although it develops at an early age, there are many factors that may limit young readers' ability to monitor their comprehension and which may cause poor comprehenders' particular problems with the identification of some types of errors in text. The techniques that we have reviewed aim to engage young readers and listeners to think about meaning as they process text, and this is probably why they benefit monitoring performance.

Glossary

Comprehension monitoring: The term used to describe what readers do when they reflect on how well they understand what they are reading.

Fix-up strategies: These strategies are not a component of comprehension monitoring; rather they are something that skilled comprehenders apply when they detect a miscomprehension, such as re-reading, checking the meaning of a word, making a valid inference.

Error detection: This is a technique favoured by researchers to assess children's comprehension monitoring ability. Errors are deliberately inserted into text and children's ability to detect those errors is measured.

Standards of monitoring: Readers may adopt different standards when they monitor their comprehension. This may depend on the task, for example reading for pleasure vs. learning from a text, and also on the individual reader's focus on the text, for example, checking that the words are known, or that the ideas in the text cohere, or how the information presented in the text fits with what is already known about that topic.

Suggested answers to activities

Activity 8.1 Spot the errors. Examples of assessments of comprehension monitoring

A   Non-word: *fod*

B   A sentence has both syntactic and semantic incongruence: "make a bid of two spades were left in the shed".

C   Internal inconsistency: Neither fried nor raw eggs can be peeled and sliced (necessary background knowledge).

D   External inconsistency: Rain worsens the conditions for snowboarding (necessary background knowledge).

E   No error but the example may need some explanation.

Activity 8.2 Spot the inconsistencies
This activity is discussed in the main text.

Activity 8.3 Dialogues to support comprehension monitoring
The question: What made the noise in the grass?

Child A: I don't know. Perhaps there was a dog?

Teacher: Can you find the place in the text where it says *cracking* noise? Try to read on a little bit.

Child B: What was the thing called – the water boatman?

Teacher: Find the places in the text where the water boatman is mentioned. Where was the water boatman when Al heard the noise?

Child C: Wayne stepped on something like a branch.

Teacher: What else could Wayne have stepped on? Have another look at the beginning of the story and try to find other things that could be in the grass.

9

PULLING IT ALL TOGETHER

"If you can read this, thank a teacher."
Anonymous teacher

The purposes of this chapter are:

- to support the implementation of current knowledge of reading comprehension in standard classroom practice,
- to focus on the construction of a mental model of the text as the focus of attention,
- to demonstrate that different component processes should be taught as needed in combination and in a flexible manner,
- to encourage the reader to make use of the ideas and information from the previous chapters.

Teaching the goal directly: the construction of a mental model

As illustrated in Chapters 1 and 2, successful comprehension involves the construction of a clear, complete, and integrated representation of the meaning of a text: a mental model of the text (Johnson-Laird, 1983). Clearly, successful comprehension can only be achieved if the reader has this goal. It is likely that good and poor comprehenders may have different goals for reading. As discussed in Chapter 4, although poor comprehenders and younger children are capable of generating inferences, they simply do not generate enough appropriate inferences to ensure adequate comprehension of text (Cain & Oakhill, 1999). In addition, relative to good comprehenders, poor comprehenders are less likely to adapt their style of reading to meet different task aims (Cain, 1999): they are less flexible readers. For example, good comprehenders take more time to read and study the text if they are forewarned that they will be asked questions after reading compared to an instruction to skim read to find the name of a character; in contrast, poor comprehenders spend the same amount of time reading regardless of instructions. In addition, when asked to describe good and poor readers in their class, responses indicate that poor comprehenders tend to view reading as a word decoding activity, whereas good comprehenders view reading as a meaning making activity (Cain, 1999; Yuill & Oakhill, 1991). Together, these findings indicate that good and poor comprehenders differ not just in their ability to comprehend, but also in their view of the purpose of reading.

If good and poor comprehenders regard the purpose of reading differently, it is likely that they will set different standards for comprehension. After all, if reading is all about "getting the words right" then a high standard for comprehension will not be set. In other words, they have a low "standard for coherence" (e.g. Perfetti, Landi, & Oakhill, 2005; van den Broek & Kremer, 1999; van den Broek, Risden, & Husebye-Hartman, 1995) and do not expect to form a clearly coherent and sensible mental model of the text.

Obviously, lower standards for coherence are reflected in lower quality of most of the component processes of reading comprehension that we have outlined in the preceding chapters. If it does not matter much to the reader whether the mental model makes sense, then the reader will see no point in struggling with inference making, comprehension monitoring, or understanding the structure of the text, and they will not appreciate that the text should fit (to a certain extent) with their background knowledge of a topic. As a result, all of the components of comprehension will suffer from the limited aim to comprehend.

Thus, one broad aim of comprehension training programmes may be to teach students to set higher aims for comprehension. Teaching a higher "standard for coherence" is unlikely to make much sense to children. They will need *reasons* to set higher aims and the most obvious reason lies in a well-defined *purpose* for reading. We expand on this idea next.

Reading for a purpose

We read for different purposes. Sometimes readers choose to read simply to be engaged and entertained. For instance, they may pick up a novel by an author they know or one that has been recommended by a friend, without having any other purpose than to enjoy the story. In school, on the other hand, reading is more often for learning, and the purposes are both more diverse and less predictable.

It is a common misunderstanding that good readers understand and remember *everything* in a text they have read. Even the best readers depend on a reading purpose, a perspective on the text. For example, Pichert and Anderson (1977) asked skilled adults readers to read a short text from the perspective of either a house buyer or a burglar. They were then asked to recall the text, both immediately and one week later. At both time points, recall was strongly biased towards the reading perspective, even though the instruction was to recall the text as a whole. So, for instance, people reading the text from a house buyer perspective were much more likely to recall information such as the fact that the living room was newly painted and that the basement was damp and musty, whereas those reading from a burglar perspective were more likely to recall facts such as the side door was always left open, and information about where the owners kept their valuables. The results showed that, in the longer term, readers only remember the details that were relevant to their reading purpose.

One broad aim of teaching reading comprehension is thus to focus on the expected outcomes of reading. The teacher can ask questions to be answered through reading, or the children can be taught to ask their own questions – a core component in "reciprocal teaching" (Rosenshine, Meister, & Chapman, 1996; Spörer, Brunstein, & Kieschke, 2009). In Chapter 4 on inferences, we discussed how different types of question could be used to assess the ability to generate inferences, and in Chapter 5 we demonstrated how different types of vocabulary question can be used to tap into different levels of vocabulary knowledge about the same word. However, here we are suggesting that questions can have another purpose: they can also be used before or during reading activities to set up clear criteria for the quality of the reading outcome. There is evidence that questions work in this way: both activities have been found to be effective in several training studies (see e.g. National Reading Panel, 2000).

The type of question is important. When teachers or students ask questions before, during, or after reading, the expected quality of reading comprehension is determined by the questions. So if the questions are about simple, verbatim details of the text, there will be no strong demands for a high-quality mental representation of the text. Conversely, if the questions demand inference making and attention to possible inconsistencies in the text, the demands for comprehension will be considerably higher. So the teacher (and the students) must be able to ask comprehension questions – and set reading purposes – that are sufficiently demanding to raise the aim of understanding.

Reading for a purpose involves the flexible combination of component skills of reading comprehension

In order to set reading purposes through questioning and other activities, teachers should be familiar with the components of reading comprehension that we have outlined in this book, and how they support each other in combination to aid the construction of an accurate and coherent mental model. A summary of these skills is provided in Figure 9.1.

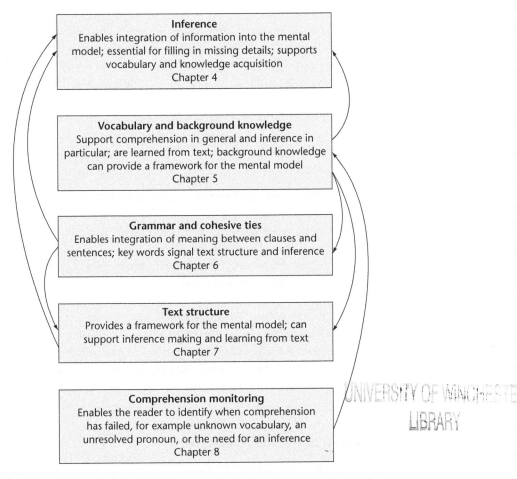

Inference
Enables integration of information into the mental model; essential for filling in missing details; supports vocabulary and knowledge acquisition
Chapter 4

Vocabulary and background knowledge
Support comprehension in general and inference in particular; are learned from text; background knowledge can provide a framework for the mental model
Chapter 5

Grammar and cohesive ties
Enables integration of meaning between clauses and sentences; key words signal text structure and inference
Chapter 6

Text structure
Provides a framework for the mental model; can support inference making and learning from text
Chapter 7

Comprehension monitoring
Enables the reader to identify when comprehension has failed, for example unknown vocabulary, an unresolved pronoun, or the need for an inference
Chapter 8

FIGURE 9.1 Some examples of the relations between components of reading comprehension.

We have not included arrows to show the linkages between all of these different skills: the diagram would get too crowded. Instead, here are just a few examples to illustrate what we mean by skills working in combination:

- When children *monitor for meaning*, they will be aware that they do not know the meanings of unfamiliar words (*vocabulary*), and may engage in *inference making* from context to work out an appropriate meaning. In this way, they will have a better understanding of the text and will also acquire knowledge from the text.
- When children draw on their knowledge of (narrative) *text structure* when reading, this framework can guide comprehension and lead them to generate *inferences* to understand the reasons for a character's actions, which may not be explicitly stated.
- When children understand the purpose of *cohesive ties*, they will appreciate the *structure* of ideas in an informational text and will be aware when the text invites an *inference* to integrate information.
- When children have secure *vocabulary knowledge*, this will aid an understanding of words that signal *text structure*, when to integrate (through *cohesive ties*), and will support *inference making*.

Once teachers have a good knowledge of the components of comprehension, and a good idea of how these components combine in practice to effect good text representation, they will be able to adapt flexibly to the particular requirements of individual children, depending on their specific needs. It is, after all, the teachers who teach, not books and reading materials.

In practice, the purpose(s) of reading should be discussed and clarified *before* reading. The point is that the purpose (e.g. answering questions) sets the expected level of comprehension (see Activity 9.1).

Activity 9.1 One text; different reading purposes

- Which reading purposes could the text below serve? Can you think of purposes that would only require skimming for a fact? Can you think of reading purposes that would require inferences? Which reading purposes would require comparisons and contrasts with additional texts?

  Venice (population 270,000, area 414 km²). Venice is a North-Italian city, which is located in a lagoon in the Adriatic sea. It is built on 118 small islands and is famous for its many canals and lack of cars. It has many monuments and sights from the time when the doge of Venice was the most powerful figure in Europe. The city is slowly sinking and is frequently flooded.

Teaching children to set reading purposes

Texts do not typically come with built-in comprehension questions to aid children to set their own goals when reading. As children get older, they need to learn to set their own purposes and aims. They need to take charge of their comprehension and become active readers. For instance, children can be encouraged to consider the topic of a text and what they already know about that topic before they start reading. They can be prompted to make associative links between text knowledge and prior knowledge by asking them what a particular object or action in a text reminds them of. Or they can be asked about pictures accompanying a text: to describe what they can see in a picture.

Such activities can take place in small groups using reciprocal teaching, where children are encouraged not only to respond to and discuss responses to the questions asked by the teacher, but also to generate their questions about what is happening in a text they are reading: both before reading and clarification questions after reading (e.g. *what, why, where,* and *how* questions). Such questions are very helpful in encouraging children to make appropriate inferences while reading (a crucial aspect of effective comprehension) as explained in Chapter 4 (where additional activities are outlined). All these activities work towards getting the readers more involved in understanding and interpreting the text.

Such activities are rather similar to the strategies for effective comprehension that are recommended by the US National Reading Panel in their conclusions. The National Reading Panel (2000) identified several categories of text comprehension instruction that have been shown to improve comprehension in non-impaired readers. Some of these types of instruction were concerned with reading purposes:

- question answering, where readers answer questions posed by the teacher and receive immediate feedback;
- question generation, where readers ask themselves questions about various aspects of the story;
- summarisation, where readers are taught to integrate ideas and generalise from the text information.

Of course, the teacher's role in helping children to use appropriate strategies for purposeful reading is also crucial. The National Reading Panel report addressed the issue of how teachers should support children's strategy use. The evidence showed that, rather than teaching specific strategies, teachers can help children by encouraging them to view reading as a *problem-solving task*, and helping them to think strategically about how to solve comprehension problems. So, for instance, if the skill to be taught is finding the main idea in a text, teachers could frame that as a problem-solving task and help the children to reason about the task strategically. In addition, it has been shown that it is helpful for teachers to facilitate discussions in which *students collaborate* to form joint interpretations of texts and to try to explain the processes that they are using to comprehend texts. Above all, these different techniques have a common aim: to support children in setting a standard for their comprehension and to support them in achieving that aim.

Helping the student get back on track

The components of comprehension mentioned in the previous chapters are each important for successful comprehension. As a result, weaknesses in each component are possible causes of poor comprehension. So some poor comprehenders may have problems primarily with making inferences, others may not monitor their comprehension well, and others may lack specific prior background and vocabulary knowledge. However, it is one thing to have information about what might be lacking in a poor or immature comprehender, but quite another thing to make a decision as to how best to help that child. There are further good reasons why the teaching of components of comprehension needs to be done in a flexible manner.

The processes of comprehension depend on each other and they work together as an orchestrated whole, as we illustrated above. In some chapters we focused on this interdependency. For example, it was explained in Chapter 5 how *vocabulary and inference making* are *mutually* helpful during comprehension: on the one hand, a certain level of vocabulary is required so that the reader understands the meanings of words, and a rich vocabulary will help support inference making. For example, knowing about *sleet* makes it easier to understand the traffic warning "the roads will be below freezing point in the morning, when sleet is expected". Drivers should infer that the (watery) sleet will freeze and form sheer ice on the roads. On the other hand, inference making supports vocabulary development because a reader who is good at inference making will be able to use context and relevant prior knowledge to help derive the meanings of unknown or unfamiliar words in the text. For example, a reader with no knowledge of sleet may be able to infer that it is a type of precipitation, and that it occurs in cold weather.

Similarly, a child who has not made appropriate inferences to form a coherent overall representation of a text will have difficulties with *comprehension monitoring* because there is no coherent representation of the text's meaning – no understanding – to monitor. As a consequence, the child will find it very difficult to appreciate comprehension problems and failures because, for such a child, a failure to understand is the rule rather than the exception. So the quality of comprehension monitoring depends on the quality of the mental representation of the text. However, the opposite is also true: the quality of the mental model of the text depends on comprehension monitoring (as laid out in Chapter 8). When the gradual construction of a mental representation is subjected to the quality control of comprehension monitoring, comprehension is improved.

Consequently, the teacher needs to consider not only which comprehension skills a child will benefit from most, but also how those might fruitfully be combined with other skills to develop that child's comprehension overall. These are important reasons why this book does not present the field of teaching reading comprehension from the perspective of various training programmes. The teacher needs to know about the component processes of reading comprehension to teach them *when they are relevant*, not in a fixed order.

Helping the student get back on track: assessing and scaffolding comprehension

Here and in previous chapters, we have discussed how questions can be used to assess comprehension: they provide a window into children's understanding of text. Therefore, a single question rarely taps a single component skill. A consideration of the requirements posed by different questions is one way to appreciate the need for a flexible use of comprehension components. Consider the following mini-text:

Leanne was waiting at the airport for her friend Khalil. The list of arrivals was showing his flight, but not the arrival time that he had sent her.

Question 1: Whose friend is Khalil?

To answer this simple question, the reader will have to resolve the anaphoric reference from "her friend" back to Leanne. Thus, the reader will have to maintain local cohesion.

Question 2: How will Khalil get to the airport?

The reader will have to maintain coherence by means of lexical links between "airport", "his flight", and "arrival time" and the likely conclusion that Khalil will arrive by plane.

Question 3: Do you think that Leanne is too late or too early to meet Khalil? This question is considerably more difficult to answer. First, the reader needs to integrate information from the text with background knowledge of airports to set up global coherence and a mental model of the situation: Leanne is in the arrivals hall looking at an information screen with arriving flights. There is a mismatch between the arrival time given on the screen and the time Khalil has sent her. If Khalil arrived much earlier than he had told her, his flight would no longer be listed on the screen. So Leanne's wait will either be a bit shorter (unlikely) or somewhat longer (more likely) than anticipated.

The above text illustrates the role of questions to assess comprehension, and also how different component skills combine to achieve good comprehension. Questioning is also a useful technique to guide the construction of meaning, as illustrated in Activity 9.2.

Activity 9.2 Different problems; different types of support

The class has read the text below. Some of the children have problems understanding it and so the teacher enters into dialogues with each of the children. Continue each of the dialogues below in ways that may provide each child with a scaffold for comprehension of the text.

The text: Clara looked up at the ceiling and sought out her favourite stain, the blotchy brown one that looked like a hen. She knew that the days of her hen were numbered because her mother had called a roofer and a decorator to do the repairs. Clara did not wish to go to sleep just yet. Her hen winked an eye and gently shook its feathers.

Teacher: What do you think made the blotchy brown stain on the ceiling?
Child A: Perhaps Clara made a mess.
Teacher: That is possible. Clara's mother calls a roofer to do repairs. So something could also be wrong with the roof.
Child A: It could be the wrong colour or something?

- How can the teacher assess the relevant *background knowledge* of the child and provide support to connect roof repairs with stains on the ceiling?

Teacher: Why has Clara's mother called for a roofer and a decorator?
Child B: Dunno.

Teacher: Do you know what a roofer does?
Child B: Is it a sort of chicken that crows?

- How can the teacher assess the *vocabulary knowledge* of the child and provide support?

Teacher: Where do you think Clara is?
Child C: Erm, at school?

- How can the teacher support the child in *making inferences* from "looking up at the ceiling" and "to go to sleep" in order to establish where Clara is?

Teacher: Do you think that Clara's hen was a real one?
Child D: Yes, it winked and shook its feathers.
Teacher: Can you find the place in the text when the hen was *first* mentioned?
Child D (finds the first lines and reads): Oh, it is just a stain that *looks like* a hen!
Teacher: Yes, so why do you think that it moves?
Child D: It says that it did. It just said so.

- How can the teacher engage the child in resolving this apparent inconsistency? And how does the teacher assess the child's awareness of Clara's point of view and what can be inferred about Clara?

Summary

In this chapter, many of the ideas of the previous chapters are brought together to provide general guidelines about how the teacher can use what he/she knows about comprehension processes to guide the child to become a more effective comprehender. Some suggestions are provided for particular activities that can be used to support and improve comprehension skills, but a crucial point is that the teacher should have a sound understanding of relevant processes and how they work together in the formation of a mental representation of the text, so that he/she can respond flexibly and knowledgeably, in order to adapt their teaching to the needs of a particular child.

Suggested answers to activities

Activity 9.1 One text; different reading purposes
- The short, informative text about Venice can serve many purposes, for example:
  - Skimming for a fact: How big is Venice? What is it famous for?
  - Purposes that would require inferences: How do you get around in Venice? Islands and no cars suggest sailing and walking. What sort of footwear would

you bring with you on a trip to Venice? (The absence of cars suggests walking a lot; and frequent flooding suggests that waterproof boots might be useful.)

- Comparisons and contrasts with additional texts: When was the heyday of Venice? Another text is needed to know when it was that Venice ruled the Mediterranean. What is being done to preserve Venice? Again, this would be the topic of a different text with a different focus.

Activity 9.2 Different problems; different types of support

- Child A. How can the teacher assess the relevant background knowledge of the child and provide support to connect roof repairs with stains on the ceiling?

  Chapter 5 on vocabulary provides information about the links between background knowledge and comprehension. The child may explore a cross-sectional picture of a house and provide the names for the different parts. An important question is whether the child distinguishes between a roof and a ceiling. It is also important to discuss in which ways damage to the roof (leaks) may damage the ceiling underneath.

- Child B. How can the teacher assess the vocabulary knowledge of the child and provide support?

  Chapter 5 on vocabulary is also relevant here. It may be helpful for the child to explore the lexical-morphological link between roof and roofer. The child can do so if reminded of better-known word pairs such as paint and painter, sing and singer. The nominal -er ending means "someone who does" paint or sing or what the verbal root refers to. So a roofer is generally "someone who does roofs". Further exploration of various roof jobs may be necessary.

- Child C. How can the teacher support the child in making inferences from "looking up at the ceiling" and "to go to sleep" in order to establish where Clara is?

  Chapter 4 on inferences during reading is particularly relevant here. One way to progress would be to ask the child to form links between various activities and where they usually take place. Where do you go shopping? Where do you eat breakfast? Where do you usually go to sleep? The child could also be asked to describe what s/he can see in different positions: standing, sitting down, lying on one side, lying on his or her back.

- Child D. How can the teacher engage the child in resolving this apparent inconsistency? And how does the teacher assess the child's awareness of Clara's point of view and what can be inferred about Clara?

  Both comprehension monitoring (see Chapter 8) and inference making (Chapter 4) are central processes here. First, it is necessary that the child realises that there is a conflict: a stain cannot move, and yet the text says that the hen moves. Next, the question is how the conflict can be resolved. The necessary inferences about Clara's point of view are quite demanding because they build on experiences of mental states, i.e. the fusion of perceptions and imaginations at the brink of sleep. To scaffold such inferences, the teacher may first draw the child's attention to the fact that Clara holds the point of view. This is perhaps most easily seen if the child is asked to describe the scene as seen from Clara's mother's point of view – or some other point of view.

Then it may be necessary to draw the child's attention to various mental states and how they affect perception. For example, being scared of the dark may turn perfectly harmless shadows into frightening animals or things. Or, looking at things in bright light through half-closed eyes may produce very attractive images. Likewise, dozing off can create a fusion of perceptions and imagination: the perception of a pattern may extend into an imagined series of events.

REFERENCES

Anderson, R. C., Stevens, K. C., Shifrin, Z., & Osborn, J. H. (1978). Instantiation of word meanings in children. *Journal of Literacy Research, 10*(2), 149–157.

Arnold, J. E., Brown-Schmidt, S., & Trueswell, J. (2007). Children's use of gender and order-of-mention during pronoun comprehension. *Language and Cognitive Processes, 22*(4), 527–565.

Baddeley, A. D. (1986). *Working memory*. Oxford: Oxford University Press.

Baddeley, A. D. (1996). *Your memory: A user's guide* (3rd ed.). London: Prion Books.

Baddeley, A. D., & Hitch, G. J. (1974). Working memory. In G. A. Bower (Ed.), *Recent advances in learning and motivation* (Vol. 8, pp. 47–90). New York: Academic Press.

Baker, L. (1984). Spontaneous versus instructed use of multiple standards for evaluating comprehension: Effects of age, reading proficiency, and type of standard. *Journal of Experimental Child Psychology, 38*(2), 289–311.

Barnes, M. A., & Dennis, M. (1998). Discourse after early-onset hydrocephalus: Core deficits in children of average intelligence. *Brain and Language, 61*(3), 309–334.

Barnes, M. A., Dennis, M., & Haefele-Kalvaitis, J. (1996). The effects of knowledge availability and knowledge accessibility on coherence and elaborative inferencing in children from six to fifteen years of age. *Journal of Experimental Child Psychology, 61*(3), 216–241.

Barzillai, M., Morris, R., Lovett, M., & Wolf, M. (2010). Poster presented at the annual meeting of the Society for Scientific Studies in Reading.

Bast, J., & Reitsma, P. (1998). Analyzing the development of individual differences in terms of Matthew effects in reading: Results from a Dutch longitudinal study. *Developmental Psychology, 34*(6), 1373–1399.

Beck, I. L., & McKeown, M. G. (2001). Inviting students into the pursuit of meaning. *Educational Psychology Review, 13*(3), 225–241.

Beck, I. L., McKeown, M. G., & Kucan, L. (2005). Choosing words to teach. In A. Hiebert & M. Kamil (Eds.), *Teaching and learning vocabulary: Bringing research to practice* (pp. 209–222). Mahwah, NJ: Erlbaum.

Beck, I., Perfetti, C., & McKeown, M. (1982). Effects of long-term vocabulary instruction on lexical access and reading comprehension. *Journal of Educational Psychology, 74*, 506–521.

Bentin, S., Deutsch, A., & Liberman I. Y. (1990). Syntactic competence and reading ability in children. *Journal of Experimental Child Psychology, 48*, 147–172.

Best, R. M., Floyd, R. G., & McNamara, D. S. (2008). Differential competencies contributing to children's comprehension of narrative and expository texts. *Reading Psychology, 29*(2), 137–164.

Biemiller, A. (2005). Size and sequence in vocabulary development: Implications for choosing words for primary grade vocabulary instruction. In A. Hiebert & M. Kamil (Eds.), *Teaching and learning vocabulary: Bringing research to practice* (pp. 223–242). Mahwah, NJ: Erlbaum.

Biemiller, A., & Boote, C. (2006). An effective method for building meaning vocabulary in primary grades. *Journal of Educational Psychology, 98*(1), 44–62.

Bishop, D. V. M. (1983). *Test for the reception of grammar.* Manchester: Chapel Press.

Bishop, D. V. M. (1997). *Uncommon understanding: Development and disorders of language comprehension in children.* Hove: Psychology Press.

Bishop, D. V. M. (2001). *Uncommon understanding: Development and disorders of language comprehension in children* (reprinted ed.). Hove: Psychology Press.

Blewitt, P., Rump, K. M., Shealy, S. E., & Cook, S. A. (2009). Shared book reading: When and how questions affect young children's word learning. *Journal of Educational Psychology, 101*(2), 294–304.

Bloom, L., Lahey, M., Hood, L., Lifter, K., & Fiess, K. (1980). Complex sentences: Acquisition of syntactic connectives and the semantic relations they encode. *Journal of Child Language, 7*(2), 235–261.

Bormuth, J. R. (1967). *Cloze readability procedure* (CSEIP Occasional Report 1). Los Angeles, CA: University of California.

Bowers, P. N., & Kirby, J. R. (2010). Effects of morphological instruction on vocabulary acquisition. *Reading and Writing, 23*(5), 515–537.

Bowers, P. N., Kirby, J. R., & Deacon, S. H. (2010). The effects of morphological instruction on literacy skills: A systematic review of the literature. *Review of Educational Research, 80*(2), 144–179.

Brady, S. A. (2011). Efficacy of phonics teaching for reading outcomes: Indications from post NRP research. In S. A. Brady, D. Braze, & C. A. Fowler (Eds.), *Explaining individual differences in reading: Theory and evidence* (pp. 69–96). New York: Psychology Press.

Bransford, J. D., & Johnson, M. K. (1972). Contextual prerequisites for understanding: Some investigations of comprehension and recall. *Journal of Verbal Learning and Verbal Behavior, 11*(6), 717–726.

Cain, K. (1996). Story knowledge and comprehension skill. In C. Cornoldi & J. Oakhill (Eds.), *Reading comprehension difficulties: Processes and remediation* (pp. 167–192). Mahwah, NJ: Lawrence Erlbaum Associates.

Cain, K. (1999). Ways of reading: How knowledge and use of strategies are related to reading comprehension. *British Journal of Developmental Psychology, 17*(2), 293–309.

Cain, K. (2003). Text comprehension and its relation to coherence and cohesion in children's fictional narratives. *British Journal of Developmental Psychology, 21*(3), 335–351.

Cain, K. (2007). Syntactic awareness and reading ability: Is there any evidence for a special relationship? *Applied Psycholinguistics, 28*(4), 679–694.

Cain, K., & Nash, H. M. (2011). The influence of connectives on young readers' processing and comprehension of text. *Journal of Educational Psychology, 103*(2), 429–441.

Cain, K., & Oakhill, J. V. (1999). Inference making and its relation to comprehension failure. *Reading and Writing: An Interdisciplinary Journal, 11*(5–6), 489–503.

Cain, K., & Oakhill, J. V. (2006). Profiles of children with specific reading comprehension difficulties. *British Journal of Educational Psychology, 76*(4), 683–696.

Cain, K., & Oakhill, J. V. (2011). Matthew effects in young readers: Reading comprehension and reading experience aid vocabulary development. *Journal of Learning Disabilities, 44*(5), 431–443.

Cain, K. & Oakhill, J. V. (in press). Reading comprehension and vocabulary: Is vocabulary more important for some aspects of comprehension? *L'Année Psychologique / Topics in Cognitive Psychology.*

Cain, K., Oakhill, J. V., Barnes, M. A., & Bryant, P. E. (2001). Comprehension skill, inference making ability and their relation to knowledge. *Memory and Cognition, 29*(6), 850–859.

Cain, K., Oakhill, J. V., & Bryant, P. E. (2004). Children's reading comprehension ability: Concurrent prediction by working memory, verbal ability, and component skills. *Journal of Educational Psychology, 96*(1), 671–681.

Cain, K., Oakhill, J. V., & Lemmon, K. (2004). Individual differences in the inference of word meanings from context: The influence of reading comprehension, vocabulary knowledge, and memory capacity. *Journal of Educational Psychology, 96*(4), 671–681.

Cain, K., Oakhill, J. V., & Lemmon, K. (2005). The relation between children's reading comprehension level and their comprehension of idioms. *Journal of Experimental Child Psychology, 90*(1), 65–87.

Cain, K., Patson, N., & Andrews, L. (2005). Age- and ability-related differences in young readers' use of conjunctions. *Journal of Child Language, 32*(4), 877–892.

Cain, K., & Towse, A. S. (2008). To get hold of the wrong end of the stick: Reasons for poor idiom understanding in children with reading comprehension difficulties. *Journal of Speech, Language, and Hearing Research, 51*(6), 1538–1549.

Cain, K., Towse, A. S., & Knight, R. S. (2009). The development of idiom comprehension: An investigation of semantic and contextual processing skills. *Journal of Experimental Child Psychology, 102*(3), 280–298.

Carney, J. J., Anderson, D., Blackburn, C., & Blessing, D. (1984). Preteaching vocabulary and the comprehension of social studies materials by elementary school children. *Social Education, 48*(3), 195–196.

Carroll, J. B. (1993). *Human cognitive abilities: A survey of factor-analytic studies.* New York: Cambridge University Press.

Catts, H. W., Compton, D., Tomblin, J. B., & Bridges, M. S. (2012). Prevalence and nature of late-emerging poor readers. *Journal of Educational Research, 104*(1), 166–181.

Catts, H. W., Hogan, T. P., & Adlof, S. M. (2005). Developmental changes in reading and reading disabilities. In H. W. Catts & A. G. Kamhi (Eds.), *The connections between language and reading disabilities* (pp. 25–40). Mahwah, NJ: Lawrence Erlbaum.

Chall, J. S., Jacobs, V. A., & Baldwin, L. E. (1990). *The reading crisis: Why poor children fall behind.* Cambridge, MA: Harvard University Press.

Chapman, L. J. (1983). *Reading development and cohesion.* Exeter: Heinemann.

Charniak, E. (1972). *Toward a model of children's story comprehension* (Technical Report 266). Cambridge, MA: Artificial Intelligence Laboratory, MIT.

Chien, Y. C., & Wexler, K. (1990). Children's knowledge of locality conditions in binding as evidence for the modularity of syntax and pragmatics. *Language Acquisition, 1*(3), 225–295.

Chomsky, N. (1957). *Syntactic structures.* The Hague and Paris: Mouton.

Chomsky, C. (1969). *The acquisition of syntax in children from 5 to 10.* Cambridge, MA: MIT Press.

Connolly, J. (1999). *Every dead thing.* New York: Simon & Schuster.

Coyne, M. D., McCoach, D. B., & Kapp, S. (2007). Vocabulary intervention for kindergarten students: Comparing extended instruction to embedded instruction and incidental exposure. *Learning Disability Quarterly, 30*(2), 74–88.

Crosson, A. C., Lesaux, N. K., & Martiniello, M. (2008). Factors that influence comprehension of connectives among language minority children from Spanish-speaking backgrounds. *Applied Psycholinguistics, 29*(4), 603–625.

Cunningham, A. E. (2005). Vocabulary growth through independent reading and reading aloud to children. In E. H. Hiebert & M. L. Kamhi (Eds.), *Teaching and learning vocabulary: Bringing research to practice* (pp. 45–68). Mahwah, NJ: Lawrence Erlbaum Associates.

Cutting, L. E., & Scarborough, H. S. (2006). Prediction of reading comprehension: Relative contributions of word recognition, language proficiency, and other cognitive skills can depend on how comprehension is measured. *Scientific Studies of Reading, 10*(3), 277–299.

Daneman, M., & Carpenter, P. A. (1980). Individual differences in working memory and reading. *Journal of Verbal Learning and Verbal Behavior, 19*(4), 450–466.

Davis, F. B. (1944). Fundamental factors of comprehension in reading. *Psychometrika, 9*(3), 185–197.

Davis, F. B. (1968). Research in comprehension in reading. *Reading Research Quarterly, 3*(4), 499–545.

de Jong, P. F., & van der Leij, A. (2002). Effects of phonological abilities and linguistic comprehension on the development of reading. *Scientific Studies of Reading, 6*(1), 51–77.

de Sousa, I., & Oakhill, J. V. (1996). Do levels of interest have an effect on children's comprehension monitoring performance? *British Journal of Educational Psychology, 66*(4), 471–482.

Duke, N. K. (2000). 3.6 minutes per day: The scarcity of informational texts in first grade. *Reading Research Quarterly, 35*(2), 202–224.

Dunn, L. M., Dunn, L. M., Whetton, C., & Pintilie, D. (1982). *British picture vocabulary scale.* London: NFER-Nelson.

Easley, J. A., & Zwoyer, R. E. (1975). Teaching by listening: Toward a new day in math classes. *Contemporary Education, 47*(1), 19–25.

Ehrlich, M. F., Rémond, M., & Tardieu, H. (1999). Processing of anaphoric devices in young skilled and less skilled comprehenders: Differences in metacognitive monitoring. *Reading and Writing, 11*(1), 29–63.

Elbro, C., & Arnbak, E. (2002). Components of reading comprehension as predictors of educational achievement. In E. Hjelmquist & C. von Euler (Eds.), *Dyslexia and literacy* (pp. 69–83). London: Whurr.

Elbro, C., & Buch-Iversen, I. (2013). Activation of background knowledge for inference making: Effects on reading comprehension. *Scientific Studies of Reading, 17*(6), 435–452.

Englert, C. S., & Hiebert, E. F. (1984). Children's developing awareness of text structures in expository materials. *Journal of Educational Psychology, 76*(1), 65–74.

Englert, C. S., & Thomas, C. C. (1987). Sensitivity to text structure in reading and writing: A comparison between learning disabled and non-learning disabled students. *Learning Disability Quarterly, 10*(2), 93–105.

Florit, E., Roch, M., & Levorato, M. C. (2011). Listening text comprehension of explicit and implicit information in preschoolers: The role of verbal and inferential skills. *Discourse Processes, 48*(2), 119–138.

Francey, G., & Cain, K. (in press). Effect of imagery training on children's comprehension of pronouns. *The Journal of Educational Research*. doi: 10.1080/00220671.2013.824869.

Gallini, J., Spires, H., Terry, S., & Gleaton, J. (1993). The influence of macro and micro-level cognitive strategies training on text learning. *Journal of Research and Development in Education, 26*(3), 164–178.

Gambrell, L. B., & Bales, R. J. (1986). Mental imagery and the comprehension-monitoring performance of fourth- and fifth-grade poor readers. *Reading Research Quarterly, 21*(4), 454–464.

Gaux, C., & Gombert, J. E. (1999). Implicit and explicit syntactic knowledge and reading in preadolescents. *British Journal of Developmental Psychology, 17,* 169–188.

Gellert, A. S., & Elbro, C. (2013). Cloze tests may be quick, but are they dirty? Development and preliminary validation of a Cloze test of reading comprehension. *Journal of Psychoeducational Assessment, 31*(1), 16–28.

Gernsbacher, M. A., & Hargreaves, D. J. (1988). Accessing sentence participants: The advantage of first mention. *Journal of Memory and Language, 27*(6), 699–717.

Gernsbacher, M. M., Varner, K. R., & Faust, M. E. (1990). Investigating individual differences in general comprehension skill. *Journal of Experimental Psychology: Learning, Memory and Cognition, 16*(3), 430–445.

Geva, E., & Ryan, E. B. (1985). Use of conjunctions in expository texts by skilled and less skilled readers. *Journal of Reading Behavior, 17*(4), 331–346.

Gillies, A. (2012). *The white lie*. London: Short Books Ltd.

Gough, P. B., & Hillinger, M. L. (1980). Learning to read: An unnatural act. *Bulletin of the Orton Society, 30*(1), 179–196.

Gough, P. B., Hoover, W. A., & Peterson, C. L. (1996). Some observations on a simple view of reading. In C. Cornoldi & J. Oakhill (Eds.), *Reading comprehension difficulties: Processes and intervention* (pp. 1–13). Mahwah, NJ: Erlbaum.

Gough, P. B., & Tunmer, W. E. (1986). Decoding, reading, and reading disability. *Remedial and Special Education, 7*(1), 6–10.

Hall, K. M., Markham, J. C., & Culatta, B. (2005). The development of the Early Expository Comprehension Assessment (EECA): A look at reliability. *Communication Disorders Quarterly, 26*(4), 195–206.

Halliday, M. A. K., & Hasan, R. (1976). *Cohesion in English*. London: Longman.

Irwin, J. W., & Pulver, C. J. (1984). Effects of explicitness, clause order, and reversibility on children's comprehension of causal relationships. *Journal of Educational Psychology, 76,* 399–407.

Johnson-Laird, P. N. (1983). *Mental models: Towards a cognitive science of language, inference, and consciousness*. Cambridge, MA: Harvard University Press.

Kail, M. L. (1976). Strategies of comprehension of personal pronouns among young children. *Enfance, 4–5,* 447–466.

Kail, M., & Weissenborn, J. (1991). Conjunctions: Developmental issues. In G. Piéraut-le-Bonniec &

M. Dolitsky (Eds.), *Language bases ... Discourse bases: Some aspects of contemporary French-language psycholinguistics research* (pp. 125–142). Amsterdam: Benjamins.

Kameenui, E. J., Carnine, D. W., & Freschi, R. (1982). Effects of text construction and instructional procedures for teaching word meanings on comprehension and recall. *Reading Research Quarterly*, 367–388.

Keenan, J. M., & Betjemann, R. S. (2006). Comprehending the Gray Oral Reading Test without reading it: Why comprehension tests should not include passage-independent items. *Scientific Studies of Reading, 10*(4), 368–380.

Keenan, J. M., Betjemann, R. S., & Olson, R. K. (2008). Reading comprehension tests vary in the skills they assess: Differential dependence on decoding and oral comprehension. *Scientific Studies of Reading, 12*(3), 281–300.

Kendeou, P., Bohn-Gettler, C., White, M. J., & Van Den Broek, P. (2008). Children's inference generation across different media. *Journal of Research in Reading, 31*(3), 259–272.

Kendeou, P., van den Broek, P., White, M., & Lynch, J. S. (2009). Predicting reading comprehension in early elementary school: The independent contributions of oral language and decoding skills. *Journal of Educational Psychology, 101*(4), 765–778.

Kintsch, W. (1998). *Comprehension: A paradigm for cognition.* New York: Cambridge University Press.

Leach, J. M., Scarborough, H. S., & Rescorla, L. (2003). Late-emerging reading disabilities. *Journal of Educational Psychology, 95*(2), 211–224.

Lepola, J., Lynch, J., Laakkonen, E., Silvén, M., & Niemi, P. (2012). The role of inference making and other language skills in the development of narrative listening comprehension in 4–6-year-old children. *Reading Research Quarterly, 47*(3), 259–282.

Levorato, M. C., Nesi, B., & Cacciari, C. (2004). Reading comprehension and understanding idiomatic expressions: A developmental study. *Brain and Language, 91*(3), 303–314.

Levorato, M. C., Roch, M., & Nesi, B. (2007). A longitudinal study of idiom and text comprehension. *Journal of Child Language, 34*(3), 473–494.

Lynch, J. S., & van den Broek, P. (2007). Understanding the glue of narrative structure: Children's on- and off-line inferences about characters' goals. *Cognitive Development, 22*(3), 323–340.

Lynch, J. S., van den Broek, P., Kremer, K., Kendeou, P., White, M. J., & Lorch, E. P. (2008). The development of narrative comprehension and its relation to other early reading skills. *Reading Psychology, 29*(4), 327–365.

Mandler, J. M., & Johnson, N. S. (1977). Remembrance of things parsed: Story structure and recall. *Cognitive Psychology, 9*(1), 111–151.

Markman, E. M. (1979). Realizing that you don't understand: Elementary school children's awareness of inconsistencies. *Child Development, 50,* 643–655.

Mayer, M. (1969). *Frog, where are you?* New York: Penguin Putnam Inc.

McMaster, K. L., van den Broek, P., Espin, C. A., White, M. J., Rapp, D. N., Kendeou, P., et al. (2012). Making the right connections: Differential effects of reading intervention for subgroups of comprehenders. *Learning and Individual Differences, 22*(1), 100–111.

McNamara, D. S., & Kintsch, W. (1996). Learning from texts: Effects of prior knowledge and text coherence. *Discourse Processes, 22,* 247–288.

Medo, M. A., & Ryder, R. J. (1993). The effects of vocabulary instruction on readers' ability to make causal connections. *Literacy Research and Instruction, 33*(2), 119–134.

Megherbi, H., & Ehrlich, M. F. (2005). Language impairment in less skilled comprehenders: The on-line processing of anaphoric pronouns in a listening situation. *Reading and Writing, 18*(7–9), 715–753.

Mehegan, C., & Dreifuss, F. E. (1972). Hyperlexia. *Neurology, 22*(11), 1105–1111.

Meyer, B. J., & Freedle, R. O. (1984). Effects of discourse type on recall. *American Educational Research Journal, 21*(1), 121–143.

Morpurgo, M. (2007). *The butterfly lion.* London: HarperCollins Children's Books.

Muter, V., Hulme, C., Snowling, M. J., & Stevenson, J. (2004). Phonemes, rimes, vocabulary, and grammatical skills as foundations of early reading development: Evidence from a longitudinal study. *Developmental Psychology, 40*(5), 665–681.

Nagy, W. E., & Anderson, R. C. (1984). How many words are there in printed school English? *Reading Research Quarterly, 19*(3), 304–330.

Nagy, W. E., & Herman, P. A. (1987). Breadth and depth of vocabulary knowledge: Implications for acquisition and instruction. In M. G. McKeown & M. E. Curtis (Eds.), *The nature of vocabulary acquisition* (pp. 19–36). Hillsdale, NJ: Erlbaum.

Nagy, W. E., & Scott, J. (2000). Vocabulary processes. In M. Kamil, P. Mosenthal, P. D. Pearson, & R. Barr (Eds.), *Handbook of reading research* (Vol. 3, pp. 269–284). Mahwah, NJ: Erlbaum.

Nation, K. (1999). Reading skills in hyperlexia: A developmental perspective. *Psychological Bulletin, 125*(3), 338–355.

Nation, K., Clarke, P., Marshall, C. M., & Durand, M. (2004). Hidden language impairments in children: Parallels between poor reading comprehension and Specific Language Impairment? *Journal of Speech, Language, and Hearing Research, 47*, 199–211.

Nation, K., Cocksey, J., Taylor, J. S., & Bishop, D. V. (2010). A longitudinal investigation of early reading and language skills in children with poor reading comprehension. *Journal of Child Psychology and Psychiatry, 51*(9), 1031–1039.

Nation, K., & Norbury, C. F. (2005). Why reading comprehension fails: Insights from developmental disorders. *Topics in Language Disorders, 25*(1), 21–32.

Nation, K., & Snowling, M. J. (1998). Semantic processing and the development of word-recognition skills: Evidence from children with reading comprehension difficulties. *Journal of Memory and Language, 39*(1), 85–101.

Nation, K., & Snowling, M. J. (2000). Factors influencing syntactic awareness in normal readers and poor comprehenders. *Applied Psycholinguistics, 21*, 229–241.

National Reading Panel. (2000). *Teaching children to read: An evidence-based assessment of the scientific research literature on reading and its implications for reading instruction*. Washington, DC: The National Institute of Child Health and Human Development. Retrieved from www.nichd.nih. gov/publications/nrp/smallbook.htm.

Neale, M. D. (1997). *The Neale analysis of reading ability–Revised (NARA–II)*. Windsor: NFER-Nelson.

Oakhill, J. V. (1982). Constructive processes in skilled and less-skilled comprehenders' memory for sentences. *British Journal of Psychology, 73*(1), 13–20.

Oakhill, J. V., & Cain, K. (2012). The precursors of reading ability in young readers: Evidence from a four-year longitudinal study. *Scientific Studies of Reading, 16*(2), 91–121.

Oakhill, J. V., Cain, K., & Bryant, P. E. (2003). The dissociation of word reading and text comprehension: Evidence from component skills. *Language and Cognitive Processes, 18*(4), 443–468.

Oakhill, J. V., Cain, K., McCarthy, D., & Nightingale, Z. (2012). Making the link between vocabulary knowledge and comprehension skill. In A. Britt, S. Goldman, & J.-F. Rouet (Eds.), *Reading: From words to multiple texts* (pp. 101–114). Hoboken, NJ: Routledge.

Oakhill, J. V., Hartt, J., & Samols, D. (2005). Levels of comprehension monitoring and working memory in good and poor comprehenders. *Reading and Writing, 18*, 657–686.

Oakhill, J. V., & Yuill, N. (1986). Pronoun resolution in skilled and less-skilled comprehenders: Effects of memory load and inferential complexity. *Language and Speech, 29*(1), 25–37.

Oakhill, J. V., Yuill, N., & Donaldson, M. L. (1990). Understanding of causal expressions in skilled and less skilled text comprehenders. *British Journal of Developmental Psychology, 8*(4), 401–410.

Ouellette, G. P. (2006). What's meaning got to do with it: The role of vocabulary in word reading and reading comprehension. *Journal of Educational Psychology, 98*(3), 554–566.

Palincsar, A. S., & Brown, A. L. (1984). Reciprocal teaching of comprehension-fostering and comprehension-monitoring activities. *Cognition and Instruction, 1*(2), 117–175.

Pappas, C. C. (1993). Is narrative "primary"? Some insights from kindergarteners' pretend readings of stories and information books. *Journal of Reading Behavior, 25*(1), 97–129.

Paris, A. H., & Paris, S. G. (2003). Assessing narrative comprehension in young children. *Reading Research Quarterly, 38*(1), 36–76.

Paris, A. H., & Paris, S. G. (2007). Teaching narrative comprehension strategies to first graders. *Cognition and Instruction, 25*(1), 1–44.

Paris, S. G. (2005). Reinterpreting the development of reading skills. *Reading Research Quarterly, 40*(2), 184–202.

Paris, S. G., & Jacobs, J. E. (1984). The benefits of informed instruction for children's reading awareness and comprehension skills. *Child Development, 55*(6), 2083–2093.

Perfetti, C. A. (1985). *Reading ability.* New York: Oxford University Press.

Perfetti, C. A., Landi, N., & Oakhill, J. (2005). The acquisition of reading comprehension skill. In M. J. Snowling & C. Hulme (Eds.), *The science of reading: A handbook* (pp. 227–253). Oxford: Blackwell.

Peterson, C. (1986). Semantic and pragmatic uses of "but". *Journal of Child Language, 13*(3), 583–590.

Peterson, C., & McCabe, A. (1987). The connective "and": Do older children use it less as they learn other connectives? *Journal of Child Language, 14*(2), 375–381.

Pichert, J. W., & Anderson, R. C. (1977). Taking different perspectives on a story. *Journal of Educational Psychology, 69*, 309–315.

Pike, M. M., Barnes, M. A., & Barron, R. W. (2010). The role of illustrations in children's inferential comprehension. *Journal of Experimental Child Psychology, 105*(3), 243–255.

Pinker, S. (1994). *The language instinct: The new science of language and mind.* London: Allen Lane.

Pressley, G. M. (1976). Mental imagery helps eight-year-olds remember what they read. *Journal of Educational Psychology, 68*(3), 355–359.

Pressley, M., & Afflerbach, P. P. (1995). *Verbal protocols of reading: The nature of constructively responsive reading.* Hillsdale, NJ: Erlbaum.

Protopapas, A., Sideridis, G. D., Mouzaki, A., & Simos, P. G. (2007). Development of lexical mediation in the relation between reading comprehension and word reading skills in Greek. *Scientific Studies of Reading, 11*(3), 165–197.

Pyykkonen, P., & Jarvikivi, J. (2012). Children and situation models of multiple events. *Developmental Psychology, 48*, 521–529.

Reid, J. (1972). *Children's comprehension of syntactic features found in some extension readers* (Occasional paper). Edinburgh: Centre for Research in Educational Sciences, University of Edinburgh.

Rosenshine, B., Meister, C., & Chapman, S. (1996). Teaching students to generate questions: A review of the intervention studies. *Review of Educational Research, 66*(2), 181–221.

Sachs, J. S. (1967). Recognition memory for syntactic and semantic aspects of connected discourse. *Perception & Psychophysics, 2*(9), 437–442.

Scarborough, H. (2001). Connecting early language and literacy to later reading (dis)abilities: Evidence, theory, and practice. In S. B. Neuman & D. K. Dickinson (Eds.), *Handbook of early literacy* (pp. 97–110). New York: Guilford Press.

Seigneuric, A., & Ehrlich, M. F. (2005). Contribution of working memory capacity to children's reading comprehension: A longitudinal investigation. *Reading and Writing, 18*(7–9), 617–656.

Seymour, P. H. K., & Elder, L. (1986). Beginning reading without phonology. *Cognitive Neuropsychology, 3*(1), 1–36.

Shanahan, T., Kamil, M. L., & Tobin, A. W. (1982). Cloze as a measure of intersentential comprehension. *Reading Research Quarterly, 17*(2), 229–255.

Shankweiler, D. (1989). How problems of comprehension are related to difficulties in word reading. In D. Shankweiler and I. Y. Liberman (Eds.), *Phonology and reading disability: Solving the reading puzzle* (pp. 35–68). Ann Arbor: University of Michigan Press.

Shapiro, B. K., & Hudson, J. A. (1997). Coherence and cohesion in children's stories. In J. Costermans & M. Fayol (Eds.), *Processing interclausal relationships: Studies in the production and comprehension of text* (pp. 23–48). Mahwah, NJ: Lawrence Erlbaum Associates.

Share, D. L. (1995). Phonological recoding and self-teaching: Sine qua non of reading acquisition. *Cognition, 55*(2), 151–218.

Skarakis-Doyle, E. (2002). Young children's detection of violations in familiar stories and emerging comprehension monitoring. *Discourse Processes, 33*(2), 175–197.

Smith, E. E., & Swinney, D. A. (1992). The role of schemas in reading text: A real-time examination. *Discourse Processes, 15*(3), 303–316.

Smith, S. T., Macaruso, P., Shankweiler, D., & Crain, S. (1989). Syntactic comprehension in young poor readers. *Applied Psycholinguistics, 10*, 420–454.

Snowling, M., & Frith, U. (1986). Comprehension in "hyperlexic" readers. *Journal of Experimental Child Psychology, 42*(3), 392–415.

Snowling, M. J., & Hulme, C. (2005). Learning to read with a language impairment. In M. J. Snowling & C. Hulme (Eds.), *The science of reading: A handbook* (pp. 397–412). Oxford: Blackwell.

Song, H. J., & Fisher, C. (2005). Who's "she"? Discourse prominence influences preschoolers' comprehension of pronouns. *Journal of Memory and Language, 52*(1), 29–57.

Sparks, E., & Deacon, S. H. (2013). Morphological awareness and vocabulary acquisition: A longitudinal examination of their relationship in English-speaking children. *Applied Psycholinguistics*, 1–23.

Spooren, W., & Sanders, T. (2008). The acquisition order of coherence relations: On cognitive complexity in discourse. *Journal of Pragmatics, 40*(12), 2003–2026.

Spörer, N., Brunstein, J. C., & Kieschke, U. (2009). Improving students' reading comprehension skills: Effects of strategy instruction and reciprocal teaching. *Learning and Instruction, 19*(3), 272–286.

Stahl, S. A., & Fairbanks, M. M. (1986). The effects of vocabulary instruction: A model-based meta-analysis. *Review of Educational Research, 56*(1), 72–110.

Stanovich, K. E. (1986). Matthew effects in reading: Some consequences of individual differences in the acquisition of literacy. *Reading Research Quarterly, 21*(4), 360–407.

Stein, N. L., & Glenn, C. G. (1982). Children's concept of time: The development of story schema. In W. J. Friedman (Ed.), *The developmental psychology of time* (pp. 255–282). New York: Academic Press.

Stothard, S. E., & Hulme, C. (1992). Reading comprehension difficulties in children: The role of language comprehension and working memory skills. *Reading and Writing: An Interdisciplinary Journal, 4*, 245–256.

Tannenbaum, K. R., Torgesen, J. K., & Wagner, R. K. (2006). Relationships between word knowledge and reading comprehension in third-grade children. *Scientific Studies of Reading, 10*(4), 381–398.

Taylor, B. M., & Samuels, S. J. (1983). Children's use of text structure in the recall of expository material. *American Educational Research Journal, 20*(4), 517–528.

Thorndike, R. L. (1973). Reading as reasoning. *Reading Research Quarterly, 9*(2), 135–147.

Tomesen, M., & Aarnoutse, C. (1998). Effects of an instructional programme for deriving word meanings 1. *Educational Studies, 24*(1), 107–128.

Tompkins, V., Guo, Y., & Justice, L. M. (2013). Inference generation, story comprehension, and language skills in the preschool years. *Reading & Writing, 26*(3), 403–429.

Tong, X., Deacon, S. H., Kirby, J. R., Cain, K., & Parrila, R. (2011). Morphological awareness: A key to understanding poor reading comprehension in English. *Journal of Educational Psychology, 103*(3), 523–534.

Tunmer, W. E., Nesdale, A. R., & Pratt, C. (1983). The development of young children's awareness of logical inconsistencies. *Journal of Experimental Child Psychology, 36*(1), 97–108.

Tyler, L. K. (1983). The development of discourse mapping processes: The on-line interpretation of anaphoric expressions. *Cognition, 13*(3), 309–341.

van den Broek, P. W. (1997). Discovering the cement of the universe: The development of event comprehension from childhood to adulthood. In P. W. van den Broek, P. J. Bauer, & T. Bourg (Eds.), *Developmental spans in event comprehension and representation* (pp. 321–342). Mahwah, NJ: Lawrence Erlbaum Associates.

van den Broek, P., & Kremer, K. (1999). The mind in action: What it means to comprehend. In B. Taylor, M. Graves, & P. van den Broek (Eds.), *Reading for meaning* (pp. 1–31). New York: Teacher's College Press.

van den Broek, P. W., Lorch, R. F., Linderholm, T., & Gustafson, M. (2001). The effects of readers' goals on inference generation and memory for text. *Memory and Cognition, 29*(8), 1081–1087.

van den Broek, J., Lorch, E. P., & Thurlow, R. (1996). Children's and adults' memory for television stories: The role of causal factors, story-grammar categories, and hierarchical structure. *Child Development, 67*(6), 3010–3028.

van den Broek, P., Risden, K., & Husebye-Hartman, E. (1995). The role of readers' standards for coherence in the generation of inferences during reading. In R. F. Lorch, Jr. & E. J. O'Brien (Eds.), *Sources of coherence in text comprehension* (pp. 353–373). Hillsdale, NJ: Erlbaum.

Venezky, R. (2000). The origins of the present-day chasms between adult literacy needs and school literacy instruction. *Scientific Studies of Reading, 4*(1), 19–39.

Walberg, H. J., Strykowski, B. F., Rovai, E., & Hung, S. S. (1984). Exceptional performance. *Review of Educational Research, 54*(1), 87–112.

Weekes, B. S., Hamilton, S., Oakhill, J. V., & Holliday, R. E. (2008). False recollection in children with reading comprehension difficulties. *Cognition, 106*(1), 222–233.

Whaley, J. F. (1981). Readers' expectations for story structure. *Reading Research Quarterly, 17*(1), 90–114.

Williams, J. P., Nubla-Kung, A. M., Pollini, S., Stafford, K. B., Garcia, A., & Snyder, A. E. (2007). Teaching cause–effect text structure through social studies content to at-risk second graders. *Journal of Learning Disabilities, 40*(2), 111–120.

Williams, J. P., Stafford, K. B., Lauer, K. D., Hall, K. M., & Pollini, S. (2009). Embedding reading comprehension training in content-area instruction. *Journal of Educational Psychology, 101*(1), 1–20.

Yuill, N. M., & Oakhill, J. V. (1988). Effects of inference awareness training on poor reading comprehension. *Applied Cognitive Psychology, 2*(1), 33–45.

Yuill, N. M., & Oakhill, J. V. (1991). *Children's problems in text comprehension: An experimental investigation.* Cambridge: Cambridge University Press.

Yuill, N. M., Oakhill, J. V., & Parkin, A. (1989). Working memory, comprehension ability and the resolution of text anomaly. *British Journal of Psychology, 80*(3), 351–361.

Zwaan, R. A. (1994). Effect of genre expectations on text comprehension. *Journal of Experimental Psychology: Learning, Memory, and Cognition, 20*(4), 920–933.

AUTHOR INDEX

SUBJECT INDEX

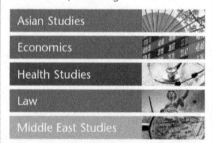
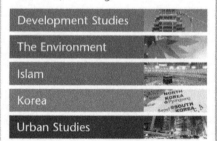